Educating for Careers

EDUCATING FOR CAREERS

Policy Issues in a Time of Change

Edited by
THOMAS F. POWERS

with the assistance of
JOHN R. SWINTON

The Pennsylvania State University Press

University Park and London

Library of Congress Cataloging in Publication Data

Main entry under title:

Educating for careers.

   An outgrowth of a symposium held in May 1976 at
Pennsylvania State University.
   Includes index.
   1.   Vocational education—United States—Congresses.
2.   Technical education—United States—Congresses.
3.   Vocational guidance—United States—Congresses.
I.   Powers, Thomas F.   II.   Swinton, John R.
LC1045.E38   370.11'3'0973   77-1639
ISBN 0-271-00511-4

Designed by Glenn Ruby

Printed in the United States of America

3/31/78 Baker & Taylor 12.50

For L.W.W.

*A great teacher never knows
how far his influence will reach.*

Contents

Preface

The period since World War II has seen two major developments in American education. First, completion of secondary education has become common; 80 percent of today's young people complete high school compared to only 50 percent in 1940. The effects of this development are many and varied, but one effect is clear: the educational ante has been raised for entry into the mainstream of America's economy. Second, while participation in higher education was confined to about 15 percent of a generation at the end of World War II, today something on the order of 50 percent of all young people participate, to some degree, in education past the secondary level. Education's growth, it must be acknowledged, was almost completely unplanned. Like Topsy, it just growed. And, as education confronted an ever broader clientele, much of its growth was in the popular career-oriented programs.

In the same period, the American economy changed. Peter Drucker has described this development as the emergence of the systematic and purposeful acquisition of information and its systematic application as the new foundation of work. While the machine was the key to increasing productivity in an earlier time, knowledge has now become the central and pervasive productive resource of our society. At the center of this development is the new work role Drucker calls the knowledge worker.

These developments are mutually reinforcing and inextricably bound together. The work force becomes better educated, facilitating the growth of technology; and an expanding "technetronic society," to use Brzezinski's term, demands a better educated worker. Further, as participation in education is extended to an ever broader proportion of the population, decisions to pursue education increasingly are consciously related to economic rather than cultural goals.

The anomalies that have accompanied increasing participation in education are numerous, but two stand out. First, while participants in education now make up the majority of society, the educational establishment to a large degree received its education in a time when higher education was an achievement of a minority only, and in a time when education was largely perceived as a cultural investment. Consequently, the newer occupationally oriented educational programs are commonly misunderstood and often despised by the most senior and respected leaders in higher education. Second, much of the leadership for the development of the newer occupational programs has come from practitioners and practitioners turned educators. The opinions of industry advisory boards and the concerns of the field of work or industry have been more consciously invoked than has the wisdom of the trivium.

Thus, unfortunately, the debate on new directions in education often is conducted in terms of, on the one hand, how to protect the liberal arts and the preserve of general education from the encroachment of base vocational interests or, on the other hand, how to improve the practicality of education, how to make it more realistic, current, and work-related. What results is not dialog but two monologs, each delivered to its own faithful.

Since policy makers often misunderstand occupational education and practitioners are concerned principally with their own programs and not broad policy, realistic debate on the educational philosophy and policies underlying this apparently new concern with vocation in education is lacking. In fact, educational policy makers and occupational education practitioners both need—and feel the need for—guidance.

To explore these general issues, a symposium was held in May 1976 at The Pennsylvania State University under funding from the Research Coordinating Unit for Vocational Education and the Vocational Education Advisory Council of the Pennsylvania Department of Education. The present volume is an outgrowth of that symposium. Unfortunately space limitations do not permit us to reproduce all the papers here.* Moreover, this volume reports only the salient arguments—the word "conclusions" would be inappropriate—rather than the full extent of the discussion. In fact, most of the discussion in this volume represents abridgements of the contributors' original work.

---

*Thomas F. Powers, editor, *Proceedings of a Symposium: Policy Issues in Educating for New and Emerging Careers* (University Park: The Pennsylvania State University, 1976). Microcopies are available from the Vocational Education Information Network, Millersville State College, Millersville, Pennsylvania, 17551.

We have organized the discussion here around three perspectives. The historical and philosophical perspective highlights the issue of agency and the roles that have been and are being played by school and industry in educating for careers. A social perspective is useful for viewing, on the one hand, the economic utility of educating for careers, and on the other, the effect on social stratification of escalating educational credentialism. Finally, curriculum design provides a useful perspective from which to explore how the fullest and best education for both work and non-work roles, for a "vocation" in the fullest sense in which John Dewey used the term, may be delivered in both traditional and non-traditional ways.

The development of this work has extended over three years. To attempt to acknowledge everyone who contributed to it would be inevitably to overlook some. But not to attempt such an acknowledgment would be presumptuous, so the attempt must be made with the knowledge that some will be unfairly left out.

Carroll Curtis, Director of the Pennsylvania Research Coordinating Unit for Vocational Education, first saw the need to move away from a "nuts-and-bolts" approach and to develop a policy view. Clarence Dittenhafer of the RCU staff provided important early encouragement. Stella Cotzen, formerly Executive Director of the Pennsylvania Advisory Council, provided not only encouragement but crucial support when, at one point, the venture nearly foundered. Her successor, Sidney Jaffe, continued that support and interested himself in the substance of our discussions. Without the generous financial support of these two agencies, the symposium and this volume would not have been possible.

Henry Johnson of Penn State's College of Education was more than a participant. He was a counselor and a friend, and he clarified my own understanding of the nature of our problem and directions for considering it. He served as the symposium's chairman, and his assistance in the preparation of the original proposal was crucial to the outline of our work. His colleagues William Toombs, Assistant Director of the Center for the Study of Higher Education, and Gary Johnson provided many insights and a good deal of constructive criticism. Theodore Vallance, Associate Dean of Penn State's College of Human Development, examined a proposal of mine for paraprofessional education some time ago and raised questions regarding some language that had Huxleyan overtones. His perceptive questions set off the entire process.

Among the symposium participants, Thomas Green and Arthur Wirth were helpful in shaping our early discussions and selecting contributors. Other participants—James O'Toole, Paul Gilmore, Lewis Dimasi, Lester Thurow, Edwin Herr, William Roark, Morgan Lewis, Audrey Cohen, George Bonham, Kenneth Tollett, Peter Meyer, Sheila Huff, Nathan Glazer, Albert Lorente, and Helen Wise, in addition to Henry Johnson, William Toombs, and Gary Johnson, whose prior contributions have been noted—generously gave their time and bore patiently with schedule changes and other administrative contretemps.

Ms. Marjorie Lawrence of the Washington State Department of Education made it possible for me to observe Project FEAST in operation.

Regarding my own contributions to this volume I acknowledge my indebtedness to my father, Urban Powers, who drew to my attention much of the material from which my thinking has evolved. In addition, Arthur Wirth, Susan Weis, and Clarence Dittenhafer were kind enough to read early drafts of my contributions critically. As a result of their criticism I was forced to clarify my views and was able to complete substantial redrafts.

John Swinton has provided more than editorial assistance. The procedure for the symposium was largely his design. John Pickering and Chris Kentera of the Press helped me understand the difference between a symposium and a book. My colleagues in Food Service and Housing Administration here at Penn State have been patient with my preoccupation with this work, and my understanding of "generalizable education" comes from my constructive interaction with them.

Rhoda and Vera Williams have typed and retyped the various versions of this volume, bearing the attendant exasperation with good humor.

Finally, I acknowledge my wife's crucial role. Without her encouragement and support, I simply would not have persevered.

Thomas F. Powers

Moon River, Ontario
June 1977

An Agenda for Debate

Thomas F. Powers

This slim volume addresses the issues of the relationship of education and work, and especially educational preparation for work, from a policy perspective. In this effort, we are responding to the burgeoning interest in career-related education at all levels of education in America.

We have adopted a policy viewpoint specifically because much of the work done in these occupational fields moves from the perspective of specific fields of work—or the perspective of educators working in those fields. The practical and technological issues of interest to practitioners are often in the foreground.

Why Policy Issues?

A policy perspective permits us to adopt a broad, societal context that sheds the potential provincialism of the practitioner, either professional or educational. The immediate cause of this study, in fact, was the discovery by one practitioner that, while he was comfortable with the "nuts and bolts" of a paraprofessional curriculum, he was at sea when he began to question the basic social assumptions on which his work was based. This realization was quickly followed by the discovery that other practitioners shared both his confusion and uneasiness.

This, then is a "practical" study that hopes to offer guidance to practitioners, and "policy" is not a code word for "theoretical as impractical," an academic exercise without meaning in the real world. In addressing policy issues, we hope to provide a basis for both reflection and action by practitioners and administrators concerned with occupational education.

Policy issues are raised, not with a view to finding *the* answers but rather, as the title of this introduction suggests, setting a framework for consideration and continuing discussion of the issues. As the writers in this volume make clear, there is a variety of views on the questions addressed. There is a considerable range of divergence, from consensus to dissensus. At one extreme, there is the fairly dramatic difference of opinion between Professors Glazer and Johnson regarding the appropriate basis for viewing liberal studies and general education. On the other hand, Professors Green and Wirth appear to be in full agreement on the issues and have simply taken different vantage points from which to view their subject. Where such harmony prevails between contributors, however, an alternate view may be presented by the editor.

Consensus on the issues is not avoided simply for the sake of discord. Rather, the divergent views encountered in this book validate Green's observation that there is no organizing principle regarding the relationship of work to education that will resolve such a problem.

What Policy Issues?

The volume is structured around several major dimensions of the problem of education for careers:

1. The issue of agency—Who is responsible for career preparation in our society and what are their roles?
2. The value of education for work—Of what use are such efforts to society? to the individual?
3. The effect of educational credentialing on our social structure.
4. The role and problems of general education in an educational world increasingly preoccupied with the practical.

While complete consensus was reached on almost nothing, some of our contributors agree that "narrow skill training" serves neither student nor employer, and that the student's occupational interest *is* a motivational tool that can be used to induce him to learn what would otherwise seem dull and irrelevant. In this context and in keeping with our goal of achieving a practical statement, a fifth section explores some basic strategies for dealing with problems in occupational curriculum planning in traditional and nontraditional programs.

Naturally, as the discussion has proceeded around these general topics, new issues have presented themselves, and these are considered briefly at the conclusion of this introduction. The volume concludes with some brief reflections on the emerging role in a changing society of occupational programs in higher education and the crucial role, there, of faculty development.

As is often the case in analyzing a complex subject, it has been necessary to abstract from reality along the lines described above. The separation of the issues is, however, somewhat artificial. The balance of this essay, therefore, will attempt a brief summary of the discussion, emphasizing the interrelatedness of the topics.

Education and Work: Agencies and Their Responsibilities

Green and Wirth address the issue of the distribution of "the social responsibilities of education *for* work and educating *through* work" from, respectively, a philosophical and an historical perspective. Green suggests that the issue must be viewed in the context of the fulfillment of a 70-year effort to make the secondary school a truly comprehensive institution. The paradox of success here is that as the proportion of the population completing any level of education approaches 100 percent—and 80 percent of America's 18-year-olds now complete high school—the relative advantages accruing from that achievement to the individual declines dramatically and the failure of attainment instead becomes a drastic penalty. Accordingly, Green suggests that in a humane future, the attainment of a high school diploma should become less necessary rather than more.

Since nearly everyone has attained a high school diploma, such an achievement "has no discriminating value for employers" and there is increasing attention to education achievement as measured by tests. There is, too, increasing challenge to arbitrary educational standards that are not rationally job related. These considerations, addressed as well by Huff in a later section, argue for a decreasing employment significance for a high school diploma and a move to exit examinations or high school equivilancy tests.

In fact, work may be in service to education as education is a preparation for work. Green points out that the more time spent in the school environment, the more limited is the student's contact with other generations, with non-school social institutions, and with experiences of productive work and responsibility. On the other hand, work as education can assist in achieving (1) independence, (2) a clarification of self, (3) engagement with others in securing collective goals, and (4) the experience of responsibility.

Given both ethical and practical grounds for decreasing our emphasis on formal education, Green suggests that it may be time for society to shift some of the burden of education to industry and other employers—and to accept the need for public or private funding of such efforts.

An alternate view which is worth considering takes account of the way institutional objectives shape the patterns of institutional policy and practice. In our society, the schools are an institution charged with educating the young in a socially responsible way. Business firms in a market society have the basic functions of producing goods and services and generating the financial resources necessary to keep the firm, as an open system, in being. This set of purposes defines a profit- and productivity-seeking entity whose proclivity for "social responsibility" is almost invariably related to its current profit position. (There is little evidence that enterprises in a system of state capitalism are any more altruistic—and some evidence to suggest the reverse.) To advocate the assignment of a role as disinterested teacher for such an organization is to refuse to recognize its defining goals and activities and to invite, at the least, discord and, at the worst, exploitation either subtle or blatant, depending on the enforcement climate. The reform and rededication of the schools seems a less Augean task than the baptism of business by fiat and fisc.

While provision at law for the protection of the right to work of educational dropouts is clearly in order, the development of education strategies credible to the poorest students have much to recommend them as a strategy to reach the 20 percent who do not complete high school. As Huff points out in a later section, in an achievement- or testing-oriented society, the poorer student and the dropout may well be worse off in that their debility will be more authentically documented.

Green suggests that America's belief that education pays will be challenged. But in a society where the penalties for not completing education are drastic, this view can at least be questioned. This question needs to be considered, however, in the light of Thurow's description of the American labor market as "internal labor markets" maintained by firms with limited ports of entry. While education clearly does not give the competence for a life's career, its significance in securing that first job and access to the training and promotion opportunity that goes with admission to a firm or industry is emphasized, too, by Huff.

Green develops the difference between job and work; Wirth takes this topic as his central issue and derives his distinction between job and work from Green and Dewey. *Job* implies simply earning a living; it is labor. Labor is seen as separate from the personal purposes of the laborer and involves low engagement of self for income he can consume with. *Work,* on the other hand, is characterized by the involvement of the worker's purpose in life, the exercise of judgment, and the sense of style and craft.

This distinction, Wirth shows, has lain at the heart of the tension between two different camps in education. The social efficiency approach to vocationalism evolved shortly after the turn of the century and took its guiding philosophy from the Social Darwinists. This ideology accepted individual differences as natural and argued for a system based on differentiation of labor that took account of these real life circumstances. Their educational philosophy argued for a "quantity production" approach to achieving universal education and the acceptance of inequality "as an inevitable characteristic." Wealth, in this view, is the natural outcome of an economic growth arising from the social efficiency of a society ordered by such a competitive and hierarchical logic. There would inevitably be inequality but all levels would achieve Gompers' goal of "more."

The task of the school in the efficiency model is to make the child an efficiently functioning unit in society. "The school in both its vocational and liberal aspects is modeled on the *job* as archetype. Schooling will sort us out according to our various capacities. As we all become more efficient in the slots right for us, we all help increase the size of the pie to be consumed." The social efficiency advocates characterized those with a less robustly competitive outlook as "simple lifers" and "romantic impracticalists."

In contrast with this view of the world, Wirth presents John Dewey's view: "The dominant vocation of all human beings at all times is living—intellectual and moral growth." Dewey clearly was not for a vocational education that would "adapt workers to the existing industrial regime." Instead, he called for "a kind of vocational education which will first alter the existing industrial system, and ultimately transform it."

Wirth's paradigm of job or work is instructive, but it may be useful to step outside it—or at least to augment it. While the concept of *work* presented is ennobling, work comes to most of us in *jobs*. The inequality the Social Darwinists exulted in may not attract us, but we have not been able to abolish it. As work comes to us in jobs and Wirth's model of jobs is essentially exploitative, then education for jobs becomes part of an exploitative system, a system of "putting vocationalism unquestionably at the service of corporate industrial needs."

An alternate view deserves consideration. If educational preparation is thought of as accommodative rather than exploitative, then it may be thought of as one means open to individuals who wish, in an imperfect world, to seek security and advancement for themselves and their children. Such a view permits the individual at least *some* choice in responding to an imperfect world.

Such a view would not, however, see the school system as the principal means of achieving greater equality of outcomes. If this becomes a goal of our society, then such a goal must probably be pursued through political channels.

Gilmore's paper suggests a point of view that may be related to this "accommodative" view of education for work. As he suggests, the long-run interests of neither student nor employers are served by a narrow, "how to" approach. On the other hand, industry *does* look for—as in his example—computer programmers who can write good technical prose (a dying art as most college professors can attest). Gilmore, from his perspective at IBM—and later Lorente speaking from a position in organized labor—notes the problems of an increasing load of remedial education in our society.

While improving education's track record at developing the basic skills of the *trivium* (logical thought and the ability to communicate and understand the communication of others) is rather pedestrian compared to Dewey's vision, remedial education would also constitute an enormously useful contribution to both students in their careers and employers in their efforts to organize the productive efforts of our society.

The Relationship of Education to Employment and Work

Our contributors in this area have adopted two different stances for viewing what vocational education is, and their divergent conclusions are shaped by their premises. Thurow reacts to "conventional vocational education" as defined in legislation prior to 1963 (and, apparently, much of current practice) while Herr examines emerging theory and practice. But a traditional organization structure of vocational education at the state level can frustrate attempts to move toward less rigid career cluster concepts in practice. As James O'Toole remarked in a recent address,

> On a practical level, experience indicates that career education is being captured by vocational traditionalists at the federal and state levels. Funds allocated for reform are being funneled through traditional sources. What promises to emerge from the new career emphasis are the same old vocational programs, only better funded and with bright, shiny new names.*

---

*Thomas F. Powers, ed., *Proceedings of a Symposium: Policy Issues in Educating for New and Emerging Careers* (University Park: Pennsylvania State University, 1976), p. 18. Microcopies are available from the Vocational Education Information Network, Millersville State College, Millersville, Pennsylvania.

Under the circumstances, Thurow's criticism of what vocational education *has been* and *is,* at much of the operating level, is understandable. He begins by asserting that we can expect high unemployment for at least the next five years. Since education does not create jobs, he concludes that vocational education is not a useful tool in addressing the problem of unemployment. There is already a surplus of skilled labor.

Thurow argues that while the conventional model of vocational education is based on the theory that the labor market exists to match labor demands with workers who have acquired skills through formal education or training, the reality is that most skills are acquired on the job. He argues convincingly that skill training and production are complementary activities, with goods or services produced in the training process sold by the employer. The actual production work setting offers the realism necessary to produce real skills and is a parsimonious training model because it produces all the needed skills without spending time on unnecessary learning. Thurow cites several studies bearing out his assertion that most skills are acquired on the job. From this, he concludes that just as it is unlikely that vocational education can solve unemployment, it is equally unlikely to increase economic growth. Since all that vocational education can do is train some people who will then displace other less skilled people, vocational education offers, he says, no social benefits.

Thurow is critical of basing vocational education policy on studies of the future manpower demand both because their accuracy with respect to any detail is highly questionable and because such studies rely on the notion that it is difficult to substitute one skill for another or capital for labor. If it were impossible to substitute one kind of skill for another, projections could be useful, but he notes that the labor market is primarily a market where supplies of *trainable* labor (rather than skilled labor) are matched with jobs. Most employers— either as a part of an industry or, in some cases, as a large single firm—"have established internal labor markets with limited ports of entry. Regardless of personal skill, there are only a few jobs at which an individual actually starts."

Internal labor markets may be thought of as comprising all the employees in a firm (or all employees in an industry where firm size in the industry is relatively small and movement of employees from firm to firm is fairly common). At the "ports of entry" workers with minimum skills—perhaps just basic literacy and computational skills—are hired for the entry level positions in which a minimum of skill is required. As opportunities for advancement occur, employees who appear to have the requisite abilities are advanced as trainees to new positions which they are asked to master. From these positions, the best qualified may, in time, receive opportunities for further vertical or lateral movement.

Similarly, within a firm or industry there may be several distinct internal labor markets. Management, for instance, may be made up primarily of persons with some college education or with bachelors' or masters' degrees who begin as management trainees and advance through junior and middle management ranks. Each position after the initial training assignment is a productive working assignment and yet may also serve the function of training the person for his next assignment. A similar grouping might be made up of technicians and skilled and semiskilled operatives.

The importance of Thurow's assertion of the central role of internal labor markets in the economy for planning occupational education programs is difficult to overstate. The key point Thurow makes is that what employers want is *trainable* employees at the entry level, employees who are equipped to participate in the continuous skill creation process of the internal labor market at a minimum of cost. As Thurow says, "If you think of internal labor markets as places where a significant fraction of all skills will be created and where most job opportunities are distributed, the goal of occupational education is to get their graduates into internal labor markets that offer significant career training." Thurow's discussion is a useful statement of the *economic* argument against a narrow skill focus for occupational education. It can complement the philosophical statement Green and Wirth, with Dewey, have made on the same subject.

Herr chooses to view vocational education in terms of the stirrings of the present and the likely shape of the future (without, however, showing that the new models of vocational education *will* win acceptance). Like Thurow, he is critical of vocational education labor market information systems as a basis for planning. Such models, he notes, in addition to the problems of forecasting accuracy discussed by Thurow, overstate the desire of all persons to work or to accept what jobs are available and do not account for sources of variance in employability other than those related to income or pay. (In "Occupational Curricula and 'Generalizable' Education" I attempt to show a constructive approach to modeling a future labor force.)

Herr rejects Thurow's criticism of occupational education as an effort to prepare fully polished, skilled workers for the labor force because, he implies, this argument is a straw man. Vocational education does not have such a goal and has been evolving new strategies since the mid-1960s.

While Herr has less faith than Thurow in on-the-job training as a source of skilled workers, he does concur with Thurow's notion of internal labor markets as a dominant economic institution. Herr emphasized the emerging use of the cluster concept and "various arrangements whereby classroom study and on-the-job experiences in local business or industrial sites could be effectively integrated." Occupational education, he suggests, is principally devoted to "providing persons with sufficient information, concepts, and skills to make them useful in many entry level positions and trainable in the specific skills required in more complex positions." He suggests that programs which will develop "behavior identified as underlying effective employability in a technological age" (in Marland's phrase) represents human capital that is virtually immune to obsolesence. The occupational education he sees emerging recognizes that failure to find or keep jobs relates more to a lack of basic literacy skills, good work attitudes, and organizational coping skills than to a lack of technical skills. At the end of his discussion, he offers a useful statement based on his own work and that of others of how academic intellectual skills and work are increasingly interrelated.

Morgan Lewis's essay offers a real indictment of detailed career planning at the high school level. The evidence he cites indicates that choices expressed in high school change for most students shortly after graduation. Indeed, a minority of vocational high school graduates in the studies he cites take their first job in the field for which they are trained and many of these subsequently leave that field. Lewis notes that this "placement failure" for vocational education is really the result of the fact that vocational education is often a "least worst" choice for students and is, thus, a serious indictment of *all* secondary education: "These students have had enough frustration and boredom in academic courses. Most of them have learned one thing well in these courses—that they are not the type of student who goes on to college. Everyone tells them they should finish high school, however, so the vocational courses are the least painful way of doing so." What is happening, Lewis says, is that they are engaging in career exploration—not career choice. Logically, then, programs should be structured to fill these needs, not to accomplish skill training.

Lewis offers another observation which is important in relation to Green's comments on shifting more of education to industry and in relation to Herr's notion of increasing emphasis on co-op programs. Virtually all of the good students are in co-op sites *but hardly any of the poorer students are.* The instructor feels the need to protect his reputation and that of his program in his co-op placement activities. Clearly, then, some students are not ready for even a limited trial in the adult world at this age—and for them, the services of the schools are crucial, for better or for worse.

Finally, Lewis questions Thurow's notion of "no social benefits" from vocational education. A young person is able to complete his education, which helps him avoid the stigma of being labeled a dropout. This constitutes an important, if imperfect, social good.

While the writers in this section express some differences of opinion, the areas of consensus are, perhaps, most significant for occupational educational program planning. Herr consciously adopts Drucker's model of the knowledge worker. As Drucker has said, "the way to teach a skill today is by putting it on a knowledge foundation." While Thurow identifies "trainability" as the proper student outcome for occupational education, we may translate that goal into the acquisition of an appropriate knowledge base. Both Thurow and Herr agree that the principal labor market realities are internal labor markets characterized by limited ports of entry. Finally, Lewis, in suggesting the need to avoid facing premature choice, is clearly calling for a flexible knowledge-based approach to occupational education that *prepares* the student for development rather than *fixing* that development.

A further important point of consensus is that skill training may provide a useful motivational tool to focus the student's attention on learning the generalizable skill that *will* be useful.

Education for Work, Certification, and the American Class Structure
The writers in this section show a marked and important divergence in their view. While Kenneth Tollett and Sheila Huff are clearly willing to accept (perhaps somewhat cautiously) occupational programs and the credentialing as a part of the American contemporary social scene, Peter Meyer and Gary Johnson both view occupational programs as exploitive of the student and laying the basis for rigidifying emerging caste lines.

Tollett begins by noting that it is unrealistic to expect to find a simple, elegant answer to the relationship of education, training, and certification to work and socioeconomic mobility, and he argues for "a healthy tolerance of ambiguity and pluralism" in our approach to the subject.

The context, which Tollett depicts for us, of the current interest in relating education and work has its roots in the land grant movement. This "practical" wing of American education has been given considerable impetus by recent history. America is emerging from a "psychosocial revolution" which began in the 1960s. This revolution was characterized by such developments as a change in the social relationships in the family, the feminist movement, a changing role for the church, and a general upheaval in the mores of our society. With the end of the Vietnam War and the peace movement came the onset of the worst recession since 1930. In this context students have refocused their attention on mundane issues related to material and professional success.

There have been social pressures on education related to the burden of financing education in a time of inflation. There is disenchantment with the academy brought on by the campus disorders of the late 1960s and early 1970s. Under these circumstances we have asked ourselves whether education ought not to be more practically oriented.

The escalation of the costs of higher education to the student have inevitably escalated their expectations of financial returns from their education, focusing renewed interest on occupational and professional courses of study. Finally, as the labor markets have been unable to absorb the expanding supply of educated workers, students see the advantage of a differentiation in occupational studies.

Tollett reviews several different "ideal" models of educational concepts, noting that while his sympathies are with a liberal arts education, particularly at the post-secondary level, each model recognizes explicitly or implicitly a vocational function for education. He suggests that the current interest in career education reflects a reemphasis on the socializing function of education.

Turning his attention to licensing and certification, Tollett notes the function of the license is to recognize qualification formally and to safeguard the citizen. Certification is legally designed as an assurance of accountability and as a means, literally, to warrant or license.

There is a trade-off between social rigidity and the protection of the public from incompetency and fraud. The effective expression of the determination of this trade-off in our society today is the requirement that there "must be a rational nexus between the license required and the evil it seeks to avoid." Thus, examinations must be job-related and due process imposes three requirements on the licensing process: specificity (establishment of standards and guidelines); rationality (relationship to effective practice); and fairness (procedural rules and adequate review).

While certification creates some social rigidity, it is "the inevitable outcome of the evolution of the United States toward a more highly technologized, industrialized and complex society." For the protection of the public, more and more jobs and vocations must be treated as if they were professions to ensure minimum competence and the highest standards of conduct.

Huff's paper raises, as did Green's, the issue of the shift from attainment to achievement in the form of test scores as the means for entry into work rolls. A problem of great significance and difficulty posed by this shift is that of the search for valid predictors of future performance. Huff suggests the difficulties posed for this work by the current state of the art in testing.

Huff raises an important question regarding the outcome of the move toward test-validated achievement for lower class students. "If tests were fairer and keener lower class kids would probably not be all that much better off." If those keener tests show that they have not, as we suspect, gotten as good an education as middle class students, they would still be on the bottom and "the knot would be tighter."

She outlines the strong connection today between educational credentials and employment opportunities. Particularly at the level of entry into the employment pool—a key career point according to Thurow—"the absence of a particular credential can eliminate a person from the applicant pool. He is rejected by a personnel officer—or he knows better than to apply to begin with." The significance of a "social good" in the form of a high school diploma or related certificate alluded to earlier by Lewis is underlined again, at least by current standards.

In contrast to the next two writers, Huff takes the position that it would be premature and therefore unfair to conclude at this time that career education is another breed of tracking—of keeping the lower class "lower." We must be on guard, but there are no grounds for hysteria. The "true bottom track," she says, is "general education" for those who are not college bound, and she notes that entry into a vocational program for inner city high school students is a real achievement.

The alternate view of career and occupational education as an exploitative part of an exploitative system is taken by Meyer and by Johnson, who shares Meyer's conclusion though not his Marxian frame of reference.

While society presents the function of education as providing opportunity for all and upward mobility for the exceptional, Meyer says that in practice education has tended to increase inequality and to ration opportunity. "The inherent contradiction confronting education in a capitalist society functioning under the guise of a democracy is the need to *appear* to promote equality while successfully reproducing the differentiated and unequal labor power demanded by corporations and other employers."

Viewing the education process as it affects society as a whole, Meyer charges that occupational programs train our young in college to refuse responsibility for the society as a whole and to retreat to their private consensus, thus raising an issue Henry Johnson considers in the next section. Echoing the distinction between job and work raised by Wirth and Green, Meyer suggests that one makes himself a marketable commodity by developing intellectual skills that have little to do with general knowledge.

He suggests, however, that the rising level of education, even though specialized, may offer a good deal of hope for social ferment and change: "Creative reorganization is all too easily stumbled upon in free and open team effort and exchange among persons with different forms of specialized training—even in the absence of a generalist."

Gary Johnson sees exploitation as arising from a society preoccupied with a power economy symbolized by and concentrated on money. Echoing Wirth's concern, he sees work increasingly divorced from any organic function of human purpose except those that further the power system. Individuals are lost in mass organizations—megamachines—characterized by adherence to a technological and purely rational ideal. Wherever this approach is applied, a rational process is present and "tends to bring mechanics to bear on all that is spontaneous or irrational" (in Jacques Ellul's phrase). This rationality is best exemplified by systemization, division of labor, creation of standards, and production norms. "Technique is opposed to nature."

The degradation of work Johnson sees accompanying these developments offers only exploitative work roles. "Career education, as it is now defined by industry and to certification programs in both the public and private sectors, represents no more than socialization to sterile, mindless, inhuman experience and, in fact, the process actually promotes and encourages acceptance of such a career context."

The problem for many readers may be that positions like those taken by Meyer and Johnson appeal only to those who are already convinced and are prepared to accept a utopian frame of analysis. For those, like the present writer, who remain unconvinced by this point of view, except as more or less elegant theory, these writings still have a potential function. While the theoretical (indeed, ideological) framework from which they move may be rejected by many, the specific dangers they warn of are worth considering.

Programs that relate to industry and other work settings *may*, indeed, fall into an exploitative mode that strives to attain acceptance of standards and practices which are not in the interests of the students or society. Educational programs that speak to the individual occupational goals of students may, indeed, encourage the privatization of education and the individual. We are warned of dangers that are real.

Education Beyond the Economic Model

There are important differences between the way Glazer and Henry Johnson see the role of general or liberal education in our society generally and in occupational programs in particular. Glazer accepts as inevitable what Johnson decries, though both are clearly exponents of the general and specific merits of a liberal education.

Glazer sees six factors as having destroyed our consensus of what a general education is or should be: the rise of science, a critical examination of classical sources, a more complex economy, the challenge to the western cultural heritage of non-western civilizations, a notion that direct experience should become a basic part of the curriculum, and the expansion of higher education to encompass half or more of the college-age population. To these one might add the explosion of knowledge and information inherent in the first four, which makes it literally impossible to do more than remain current in one field or a few related fields.

Glazer chronicles the "decay of the notion of a curriculum" from nineteenth-century liberal arts to a twentieth-century elective (and fragmented) curriculum held together, if at all, by some very limited distribution requirements. Several of the most distinguished liberal arts institutions have devoted considerable resources to an attempt to solve the problem of defining a liberal education, and all have fallen far short of success. If these most distinguished leaders cannot define a liberal education for their clientele, Glazer asks, how can we reasonably expect to develop a binding consensus for an educational establishment reaching half the college-age population? The question is manifestly a realistic one.

Glazer seems to advocate a "disaggregation" of education in which occupational training would be separated from other education in specialized institutions that take a "no-nonsense" approach to intellectual preparation for work. But this raises the question of whether we can separate the ethical training for work from other work-related learning. The practice of many business schools and law schools is instructive in this respect. Many such schools offer and require courses in business responsibility or professional ethics. In fact, it seems one can't disaggregate people—and practitioner ethics are a valid part of the educational endeavor because a valid part of the practitioner. Hence it may not be best to separate professional education from social institutions whose responsibility is to society as a whole rather than just to its students and a profession or industry.

Glazer presents some instrumental arguments for general education. It is economically useful to be able to read, write, and speak effectively. An understanding of the structure of government is useful and can be profitable. A knowledge of social trends helps one ride the waves of the economy. The development of an appreciation of culture supports needed recreation and enhances social interchanges. Glazer suggests that the supporters of general education (and, one suspects, Professor Glazer, as well) would reject these instrumental arguments. But again we must ask whether people can be disaggregated—whether one's intellectual life need be separated into cultural and noncultural compartments as work is socially divided, in a slave economy, between base and noble. In fact, general education's strongest suit is probably that it *is* the most utilitarian of educations.

But as purists might unanimously reject such arguments, they would as quickly fall out over the definition of just what a "purely" liberal education is. In a pluralized society and a knowledge economy, agreement appears to have become impossible. We may do well, given the purist's difficulties, to recall that utility does give some unifying coherence to the concept.

Where Glazer accepts as a given the collapse of a specific and all-encompassing notion of a liberal education, Henry Johnson expresses both alarm and dismay and issues a call for the rediscovery of consensus. Education, Johnson charges, has come to be based on private interest since the coming of the elective system. Alluding to the *Ius Gentium* which defined "how a man ought to act" he quotes Horace Mann as warning that we have, as a society, the choice of developing and teaching a binding consensus, choosing a master to obey, or accepting an anarchy of private desires in which power becomes the only ordering principle.

The paradigm Johnson derives from Mann is compelling, and yet two questions have to be asked: How shall we resolve, in a free society, where my accusation of anarchy shades into your definition of freedom? And perhaps more basically, is the development of such a consensus the principal work of the school? For Johnson, following Dewey, it is. Dewey's "new education" and its success will depend as much on social and economic change as on pedagogical reform, Johnson points out.

Surely educators will make a contribution to any discussion of a new consensus, but to undertake such an ambitious effort as a principal charge assumes education as a causal agent in society. Many will accept that assumption; but others, the present writer included, will view educational institutions principally as reflecting rather than shaping society. If they shape, it is in their role as the provider of skills citizens can translate into economic and political power.

Johnson asks if there is anything we can hold about social value. But clearly he has more ambitious goals regarding how large an "anything" he will accept as adequate than Glazer, who suggests he would not want Johnson to prescribe what he, Glazer, must agree to.

While Johnson and Glazer disagree on the degree of consensus that is possible, Lorente offers encouraging evidence that significant consensus is developing in the support of both large industrial firms and organized labor of a broader approach to education for careers in the career education model. After pointing out that much of the political clout for public education has come from organized labor, Lorente indicates agreement with Huff's designation of general education in the high schools as the real bottom track. He cites the extensive experience of his union in Manpower Training Programs in which the task was often that "of enrolling high school graduates, fresh from commencement exercises, directly into remedial programs, teaching them how to read, write, reason, and perform basic math."

While Lorente, speaking for organized labor, rejects what has been *labeled* as general education in the past, he also makes clear the UAW's firm conviction that public education *must* provide for more than merely conditioning a student with education for work. Educational experiences, he says, must always relate clearly to all of life. Learning how to learn, developing decision-making skills, developing adaptability and coping skills are all necessary parts of education. While he sees job preparation as important, cultural, aesthetic, and leisure activities are also essential.

But Lorente sounds a note of caution that echos the concern O'Toole was quoted earlier as expressing regarding the continuing power of the vocational education establishment. Entrenchment of tradition, the guarding of proprietary interests, and the lack of an all-out, well coordinated effort involving all segments of our communities are the main reasons for the imperfect response of the public educational system to the challenge of our times.

We can agree with Wise that education is doing its work more effectively now than ever before. It is also true, however, that the direction our society's development has taken suggests that even more is being and will be asked from education. While not all would agree with Dewey that education's work is to transform society to some more egalitarian form, we can generally expect agreement with Lorente and Gilmore on the need to develop basic communication and computation skills. This would mean finding the means to reach a still larger proportion of the poorer students. No one has said that will be easy—or inexpensive.

The discussion in this section suggests three bases for a minimum support for education beyond the economic model. These include, first of all, the "instrumental" dimension discussed earlier. Second, Glazer suggests there is some minimum of political and social knowledge our society demands, and this is an important defining parameter of general education. Finally, there is the unquestioned fact that, though in differing forms, the liberal arts will flourish in some institutions. This should, Glazer suggests, have society's support.

Some Further Issues

As is to be expected in a discussion of this kind, new issues are raised that were not formally a part of the original agenda. One of these involves the clearly documented need for educational programs that "package" intellectual skills in a way that is credible to poorer students. I offer some practical observations on this topic in "Occupational Curricula and 'Generalizable' Education."

A second set of issues involves the definition of education's task in terms of transforming society, as Dewey advocates, as opposed to a view of education as a publicly funded service industry responsible to society but also to its clientele, the students. The second view would see education's greatest potential for social change in providing students with intellectual tools they can translate into economic and political power. If the achievement of equality of outcomes is to become a goal of our society, this view would argue, the means lies not in the schools but in the political process—and confusing the two is not only ill-informed but dangerous as well.

Related to the previous issue is whether education for work is necessarily exploitative *because* it is in the employer's interest. Might not a more reasonable view see education for work as accommodative to the interests of students in gaining entry into key internal labor markets and to employers (and society's) needs for productive workers? The notion that such an effort is exploitative assumes that a capitalist (or power mad) society needs differentiated labor to maintain itself. The alternate accommodative view would see labor force roles as reflecting the differentiated abilities encountered in nature. One hates the thought of being a "Social Darwinist"—and yet there are some realities that cannot be gainsaid.

Finally, in a world of differentiated abilities in which even the prospect of equality of outcomes eludes us, the educational institution charged by society with a special kind of responsibility poses a dilemma—one, however, we may well choose to live with. On the one hand, as Wise points out, we ask too much of our educational institutions. On the other hand, asking less—shifting some of the burden for education to industry or disaggregating liberal studies from occupational programs—may be the kind of bold stroke that deserves long and careful contemplation before action. For all its imperfections, we may have a better thing than we know.

I
Education and Work: Agencies and Their Responsibilities

Education and Work:

Which Agency? What Responsibilities?

THOMAS F. GREEN

Between the institutions of work, on the one hand, and the institutions of education, on the other hand, how should we distribute the social responsibilities of educating *for* work and educating *through* work? Apart from the practical experience of people within the educational institutions and productive enterprises, probably no discoverable principle will provide a satisfactory answer to this question. The dimensions of the problem are constantly changing and answers are constantly evolving. Nothing, either in the concepts of "work" and "education" or even in the social organization of work in modern times, will resolve the problem once and for all. In considering the problem, therefore, we must seek a judgment balanced between what is educationally sound, economically feasible, socially acceptable, and politically workable. While the single answer is liable to elude us, we can nevertheless comment upon the dimensions of the problem itself—why it arises at this point in our history, and what its importance for American society may be.

I shall formulate and comment on three propositions that significantly define this problem. The first proposition is that the circumstances under which we are likely to question the social distribution of these educational responsibilities seriously are precisely those circumstances in which the relating between work and formal education is least effective and efficient. In short, the problem of the relation between education and work is most likely to get raised when any fresh answer is least likely to succeed.

My second proposition is that the distribution of educational responsibilities will be strongly influenced by the size of the total educational enterprise. At this point, I want to suggest that the elementary and secondary educational system, as we know it, has become about as large as it will become and may have become larger than it ought to be. And I want to defend this claim on *educational* rather than political or economic grounds. Its immediate implication is that if we expect a continuing expansion of education as a human activity, then we should not expect it to occur within the elementary or secondary system as we currently know it. The educational system must become less oriented toward work, and work must become more oriented toward the development of education. The result must be a redistribution of the social responsibility for education and a relocation of the place of education within the total array of our social institutions.

My third proposition is that for the next generation, and possibly for the next beyond that, the skills needed are less likely to be specifically job-oriented and more likely to be the skills of personal and social planning.

Consider my first proposition: Under conditions of full employment or during severe labor shortages, the relationship between education and work is unambiguous. The relationship is neither as clear nor as efficient as it can be, but it is *better defined* under these circumstances. I have in mind the ease with which people learned and entered new occupations during World War II. Under conditions of labor shortage, the educational system is most effective in its relation to work. Under these conditions, educational programs can be designed for particular occupations or sets of occupations, and the probability is high that those who attend such programs will gain employment in the work for which they have prepared themselves.

In addition, under conditions of marked labor shortages, whether people gain employment in the fields for which they have prepared educationally becomes an open question. Under conditions of full employment not only does this question remain open, but it also remains unasked. Certainly those who are employed do not wonder about it. Why should anyone else, except perhaps a scholar or a labor analyst?

During times of a labor surplus, however, questions about the relation of education to work are liable to appear. And these are also the conditions under which the educational system is least able to forge an effective link between education and work. Part of what we mean by "a labor surplus" is that many people find difficulty gaining employment in the fields for which they are prepared, no matter how well prepared they may be. Under these conditions, people tend to ask about the value of their education and about its relation to prospective work. The connection is likely to be questioned precisely because it has weakened.

It might be argued that under conditions of full employment, we do not need career education; and under conditions of substantial unemployment or underemployment, it does not do much good. This argument puts the matter dramatically but inaccurately. There are good educational reasons for the current concern with career education. But it is instructive to note with some care the historical circumstances under which the contemporary movement gained its impetus. It began with the encouragement of Commissioner Marland and with the quite legitimate concern that nearly one-third of high school graduates were prepared neither to assume their places in the employment system nor to enter traditional post-secondary education. This concern was also well-timed. It received expression almost exactly when we were confronted with the largest cohort of graduating high school students, and the largest class of college graduates, in our history. In short, it came with a dramatic oversupply of educated people entering the labor market—an experience that illustrates my first proposition.

But here is a further irony: When the utility of education for work is most problematic (that is, when we are confronted with a surplus of educated people in the work force) we inevitably respond by trying to force the educational system to prepare people for work more efficiently by creating a stronger connection between what is taught and what is demanded in the employment system. In short, we pay more serious attention to producing "marketable skills" just when we need the skills to find and secure meaningful and productive employment in something people are not prepared for. We ask education to develop specific skills just when we most need general and polyvalent skills. This approach has always proven to be inefficient. Thus again, my first proposition: We are most disposed to find a serious problem in the relation between education and work at those times when education has the least effective connection with work, and to respond to that problem in ways that are least efficient.

The seriousness of this claim is, however, discoverable only in my second proposition. The most remarkable development in American education over the past 50 years has not been the growth of higher education, even though that has received the greatest attention. Vastly more significant has been the growth and completion of the secondary system. The proportion of each generation of 17-year-olds completing the twelfth grade in the American system was about 6.4 percent in 1900, 30 percent in 1930, and 50 percent in 1940. It reached 75 percent in 1964 and began to level off. It has since become stable, fluctuating no more than 1.5 percent above or below that level. No other decade in this century has been as stable. When we examine the proportion of each generation of 18-year-olds completing the twelfth grade, the figure passes 80 percent—and is leveling off. During this same period, the average length of the school term has been extended by nearly 75 percent and has now reached the point where on the average in some parts of the country children spend as many days at school—and with less absenteeism—than workers spend on the job. This trend may also be leveling off.

We are probably witnessing, first of all, the completion of a 75-year effort to make the secondary school a truly comprehensive institution. Secondly, the institutions of formal education have gained an increasingly prominent and powerful role in the growing up process for more youngsters for more of their lives.

These developments are familiar enough even though we seldom view them over such an extended period and seldom face their implications. Those implications are devastating: First, in this process we will witness a transformation in the value attached to education itself including our views about its utility for work. Second, in the process of achieving the goals of our long-standing policy of educational expansion, we have transformed not only the value of education but also the conditions of growing up. I shall examine these two points respectively.

Imagine a hypothetical society in which all youth spend all of their maturing years within institutions we would recognize as schools. (Nobody believes that the United States educational institution is actually this powerful. But such a hypothesis as an intellectual exercise reveals what would happen as such a point is approached. In fact, we have come closer to this point than anyone would have guessed 25 years ago.)

If we ask under what conditions any society would extend the power of its educational system even as far as we have, those conditions would include a widespread belief in the relative benefits of education to the individual and the relative benefits it can secure in the work place. If education clearly pays in future benefits to the individual, then social justice requires that it be universally available at higher levels and for as long as is necessary for each individual to secure whatever benefits he can. (And here, parenthetically, you have the fallacy of aggregation.) As soon as everyone succeeds at any particular level, it follows immediately that the relative benefits to anyone completing that level fall to zero. It also follows that, as that point is approached, the relative liabilities of anyone not succeeding will escalate rapidly to the point where failure becomes a personal disaster. The social cost of such failures will rapidly reach intolerable proportions. In other words, in a society where 90 percent in each generation drop out, being a dropout poses no problem. In a society where only 20 percent drop out, it can be disastrous. Under these conditions, instead of being worth pursuing for the sake of certain goods, education turns out to be something to endure to avoid certain evils. Education becomes compulsory in ways and to degrees never intended.

This perspective is particularly poignant for minority groups. In every developed country in the world, they are the last to benefit from the educational system. And they typically seek to benefit from education in the same ways the majority has benefited. The irony is they cannot. For the majority, education was a good; for them it is a necessity. For others it paid; for them it merely helps avoid disaster. Analogously, unless the present generation of graduates confirms the belief that a college education pays, the next generation may find itself in a position akin to that of the minorities: For them there will be nothing in particular to be gained from undergraduate study, even though it will have become a necessity.

These observations imply a transformation in the value we attach to education itself, and a transformation in the ways in which we value its relation to work—that is, employment. We have always had voices declaring that education is not to be valued so pragmatically. They usually offer two arguments: The first is that education is intrinsically good. It enriches experience, expands horizons, and adds valuable but delayed leisure pleasures. As true as this argument may be, it is irrelevant to those people, often among the minorities, who find the pleasures of study, unlike the pleasures of play, too remote.

The other argument declares that education is an aggregate good for society. It produces an informed electorate and better citizens. This also is true and vitally important. But what is good for society in general is almost never a sufficient motive for anyone in particular. No youngster ever struggled to complete high school simply to improve society.

The view that education pays in terms of the individual's specific self-interest and at the workplace remains central to the American valuation of education. That view also explains our capacity to enlist political support for educational institutions. Yet it is becoming clearer that high school diplomas provide no great advantage to those who earn them and are a desperate necessity for those who do not. This transformation in values requires an entirely different kind of political argument. If it can no longer be demonstrated that education advances the self-interest of individuals, it becomes increasingly difficult to support educational institutions politically.

That traditional, almost religious American faith that education is good because it pays and that more of it is better because it pays more is being severely tested. It will not survive unchanged. And this traditional American view of the value of education is also central to the American understanding of the ways in which education and work are related. That understanding too will almost certainly lose the credibility it has had in the past.

I have been addressing the consequences of approaching universal educational *attainment* at the secondary level in the American system. Attainment should not be confused with *achievement.* Completing the twelfth grade implies nothing about what has been learned. In a society where everybody completes the twelfth grade, having done so has no discriminatory value for employers. But *how* it is completed—in what kind of program, in what kind of school, with what excellence, and with what experience—can continue to have enormous discriminatory value. Thus we are witnessing a shift in attention from *the importance of educational attainment* to *the significance of educational achievement.* It may well become increasingly unnecessary for students to complete the twelfth grade. The growth of the high school equivalency program and the alternative routes to a high school diploma in New York are signs that this development is under way. The introduction of an exit examination in California is even stronger evidence. I suspect that we will move first to alternative ways of getting a high school certificate and then to some exit examination with no attainment requirement at all. These, at least, are the implications of a shift from attainment to achievement in education.

These implications all rest on the familiar logic of "opportunity costs," or the economic principle that there is no free lunch. If A can do either x or y and chooses to do x, it follows that he forgoes doing y. The argument is the disjunctive syllogism. If society chooses to retain all its youth all the time within a certain kind of institution, it follows that society will not afford youth certain other alternatives. It means that the contact of youth with those of other generations will be limited, the range of institutions available to youth outside of school will narrow, their experiences with productive work will lessen, and the maturing experiences of responsibility will be less available. By no coincidence, this analysis illustrates my second proposition, that the distribution of educational responsibilities will be strongly influenced by the size of the total educational enterprise.

In our commitment to the advancement of educational attainment, something of this sort has already occurred. No doubt our almost universal practice of tying school financing to average daily attendance has had something to do with this long-term trend. But the important point is that in this process, society has had less need to provide settings for young people to gain whatever maturation may be associated with authentic work experience. We are out of practice in affording the educational benefits of work experiences. But we cannot protect all youngsters from the risks of hard, productive labor by holding them in the schools longer without, at the same time, depriving them of the educative benefits of this labor. But what are the educative benefits of work?

Engagement in productive activities (that is, work) is indisputably essential to the process of growing up. It helps a youngster achieve independence, clarify his image of himself, secure collective goals with co-workers, and experience responsibility.

These are the educative benefits of *work*, not the educative qualities of *jobs*. The distinction is useful. Work is a human necessity. It is the principal way human beings redeem their lives from futility and reveal their selves to other selves. A world without work would lack accomplishment and craft. These remarks do not imply a return to primitive capitalism or a simple Puritan ethic. They are intended, on the contrary, to emphasize the human need for work without regard to the form that the work may take—whether in the fine arts, in molding the civic community, in the industrial arts, or in agriculture.

But to say that work is humanely essential and developmentally necessary is not to imply that the jobs available to youth will have the maturing effect we seek for them in work. Nor does it imply that the jobs available to anyone in an industrial society can make the maturing educative contribution we seek for youth. But by failing to distinguish between the educative importance of work and the economic instrumentality of jobs, we confuse the relation between education and work. Education for work should not be confused with education for jobs.

I suggest again that there is such a thing as an optimal size for the educational enterprise at the elementary and secondary levels, and that we have passed that point. Moreover, partly as a consequence of this fact, our society has become unpracticed in providing experiences of work for youth in ways that are genuinely educative. Finally, educators, probably more than business leaders, have overlooked the difference between education for work and education for jobs. As a result, educational policy is prone to provide the wrong answers to the continuing problem of the relation between education and work (and their institutional locations), and to provide those answers in ways that are ineffective and inefficient.

I believe that we should seriously consider the possibility that there is an optimal point beyond which the system should not grow, and should not be universal. In a humane future, the attainment of a high school diploma should become less necessary rather than more, because educational achievement is already becoming more important than educational attainment. It follows that educators must discover grounds other than the relation with work on which to seek political support. On the other hand, none of these changes should be undertaken unless business, industry, and organized labor take a more educative point of view about how work is typically organized. A curriculum is, in fact, implicit in the employment structure of every American business and industry. For the most part it remains unnoticed or unexamined. If educators must learn to provide settings for youth to gain the benefits of work outside of school, then institutions and organizations of work must learn to consider in more practical ways how the work they offer can be made more educative. We the public shall have to accept the notion that unproductive time devoted to the educational advancement of people in a work setting should be subsidized either out of taxes that would normally go to the schools or from the funds of labor and business. The assumption (widely accepted in education, labor, business, and industry) that people should complete their education *before* beginning productive employment will have to be re-examined.

The present generation of students is unlikely to value its education because it leads to quick careers. Rather those students are likely to value education for the general skills and flexibility it affords them in the struggle for comfortable self-fulfillment. We support education now because we believe that it affords greater access to employment opportunities. They are likely to value it only if it permits them to create opportunities that do not now exist. We think that education *leads* to careers, and we value it for that reason. They are likely to value it only if it permits them to become the kinds of people who can *make* careers. We value the instrumental social benefits of education. They are more likely to value its intrinsic benefits.

I stress these points not to make light of the importance of acquiring those specific skills required to secure and maintain employment. Acquiring these skills is important. But they will not form the central connection between education and work for the next generation. I stress the need to develop the kind of education that prepares people to discover or create a work for their lives, not merely jobs to maintain their lives.

The relation between education and employment is only one of the two fundamental problems that educators must somehow answer for every generation. The other is the necessary connection between education and the maintenance of our common civic existence. Currently this country has no policy proposal or educational movement based on the premise that we live in a "common world," requiring definable and difficult skills for participation. What movements and proposals we have emphasize, instead, "self-enhancement" and "individualization." Neither career education nor "competency education" as they currently exist do much to develop a consciousness of a "common world," the skills required to find a place within it, or the awareness that participation might indeed be one's work—though not necessarily one's job.

The idea that someone may be a good person without being good *at* anything, good *for* anything, or good for *anyone,* is pretty strange. Being a good person within any kind of public or civic existence is a kind of comprehensive competence in itself. It requires a definable set of skills. It includes knowing how to secure certain goods in the world. (By "securing" I do not mean "getting for one's self." I mean "securing" in the sense of "making firm" or "tying down.") These goods include friendship, security, sustenance, and the worldly conditions and personal dispositions of civility, insofar as such goods can be secured against the vagaries of fate. Being a good person in this world involves knowing how to conduct oneself; knowing how to use time, talents, and resources; and understanding how things work.

Try a simple intellectual experiment: Picture the best and most complete kind of human life you can—full, abundant, and active in every good way. Now add to that image a condition of complete ineptitude. That added condition jars the image; it does not fit. Add the further condition of insulation from others. This makes the deviation from the good life all the more pronounced. This connection between being a good person and being a competent person exercising his competence in the midst of some kind of civic community is simply an integral part of our moral conscience. It has always been so. It has always been the experience of men that when the world goes to pot in a hurry, when the traditional understanding of the good life seems to fall away, when the principles on which we rest the coherence of life no longer command belief, then men turn their attention to the questions that really count: how to secure those conditions without which the good life cannot exist and the good person cannot survive; and how to secure those conditions without which friendships cannot endure, community cannot be enjoyed, and power cannot be chained to authority. The best kind of person exhibits a kind of comprehensive competence, an all-inclusive practical skill or art exercised, moreover, in the midst of a community. Anyone who would contribute to the making of a world and securing human goods within it requires this skill. And only in building that world will we discover the central meaning of human work.

This work demands personal, moral, and practical skills, not only for creating a link between the individual and his civic community but also for permitting a wide latitude in making or discovering employment. The skills needed are essentially the skills of planning and choosing that I alluded to in my third proposition. They involve learning how to pass from mere criticism to the development of practical proposals—how to decide what is good for *us* rather than what is good for *me*. They involve confronting the irony of human goods: that in the pursuit of some we inevitably sacrifice others. They include having to confront time constraints—what can be accomplished in the short run, and what can be done by patient steps in the long run. They involve learning the moral toughness to make decisions between alternatives none of which are particularly attractive and acquiring a sense of when it is best to act.

From this perspective, accounting takes on the aspect of a moral discipline and engineering becomes an extension of moral philosophy. Imagine an industrial firm with an extraordinarily large turnover. The engineer asked to design machinery for this firm can attack the problem in two drastically different ways. First, he can design a production process requiring such simple operations that any one of them can be mastered in a few minutes. Thus he minimizes the effects of the labor turnover. (He also creates a "curriculum" based on mastering insignificant principles with no lesson logically subsequent to any lesson learned.) Second, he might design an environment that minimizes the turnover itself rather than its effects. That choice is bound to produce an employment curriculum that is vastly richer. Moreover, the engineer who solves the problem this way will probably see his professional skill in relation to his job *and* see his job in relation to a life work connected with the entire community. That, it seems to me, is the kind of relation among education, jobs, work, and civic life that we should be investigating and promoting.

Job and Work:
Two Models for Society and Education

ARTHUR G. WIRTH

When I examined the debate over what John Dewey called "the vocational aspects of education," I saw that more was involved than mere pedagogical word play about whether there should be skill training programs and who should run them.[1] In the large sense, the debate was over what kind of society we want under technological conditions, and what qualities should mark the education of our young. The social efficiency philosophers like David Snedden and Charles Prosser generally favored social policies and approaches to schooling that would support the dominant values of the emerging industrial corporate system. Dewey and like-minded progressives were committed to challenging some of the dominant values and redesigning the institutions of society.

As I became familiar with Thomas Green's views on the relationship between education and work, I saw that some of the policy questions at issue in that early round relate to his concepts. I plan to focus sharply on ideas relevant to his distinctions between "job" or "labor" as opposed to "work," which he developed first in *Work, Leisure and the American Schools*. I shall offer the (oversimplified) argument that the two philosophies divide sharply between "job" and "work" orientations. This split shows in different ideas about what the good society should be and how to get it, and in different images of what good schools should be. "Job" and "work," in effect, become two models—for society and education.

The differences appear, for example, in Green's remark that "in the modern world, the sphere of 'labor' has been enlarged and the sphere of 'work' diminished."[2] Snedden and Prosser would view that development with favor. Dewey viewed it with dismay.

We need to have before us the distinctions between job or labor and work. It would be impossible for me to replicate them as a preface to my discussion, so I am confined to the briefest and crudest précis of Green's position.

Green feels it is useful to distinguish job and labor from work along these lines: Having a "job" in the most basic sense is to have a way of making a living. If the living is made by "labor" alone it includes features like doing tasks separated from a sense of completion or fulfillment in some object. Labor is separate from the personal purposes of the laborer, and it involves production of items primarily to be consumed rather than to be put to use in people's lives. It involves a low engagement of self; its goal is income one can consume with.

"Work," as Green uses the term, is quite different. It includes dimensions like producing stable products that enrich or sustain life, and in which the worker's purposes and meanings are involved. A job becomes work when its performance involves qualities like "exercise of judgment, a sense of style, and the practice of craft."[3] A person's quest for work is related to the human quest for potency in which one may explore his potential, test his limits, be in touch with his powers, and in the process discover his dignity and worth. Green described the society in which the possibilities are maximized for every person to find work as a "leisure society." In important respects, Green's leisure society is close to Dewey's idea of a democratic society. Green's and Dewey's conceptions of the good society both differ from that of the social efficiency philosophers with their emphasis on "maximizing production and consumption" as the primary mark of a good society.

The Social Efficiency Approach to Vocationalism

Among the early proponents of vocational education in the 1890s were representatives of the business community. The National Association of Manufacturers, for example, was founded in 1895. Its leaders were motivated in part by the need to increase their share of foreign markets and thus to overcome the depression of 1893. They felt they needed to increase their production efficiency, but they still found it difficult to meet the challenge of their chief competitor, Imperial Germany. When they investigated the sources of German achievement, they discovered highly differentiated vocational training programs geared precisely to the hierarchical skill needs of German industry. This was, of course, a system separate from the general schools directed by the Ministry of Commerce—in other words, the Germans had a "dual system."

These American businessmen believed that the social Darwinist philosophy of William Graham Sumner expressed the source of human progress. This ideology assumed that society consists of isolated individuals of varying abilities and capacities. Left to advance their own interests in rugged competition, they would bring material plenty for all. From this wellspring of increased production and consumption would flow all other goods—a home of one's own; more education for the children; and support for religion, philanthropies, and the arts.

Perceptive leaders operating from these premises were aware that new corporate-technological economic conditions were emerging and that they were based on increased rationalization of production and specialization of job functions. The logic of social Darwinism for vocational education was clear. Its task was to increase material productivity as vocationalism had in Germany, to meet hierarchical skill needs, and to instill attitudes and training that preserved the dominant values of the social Darwinist ideology. "Social efficiency" and "social control" were the watchwords. Ideally the logic called for a set of separate vocational schools, guided by men of industry and patterned on the German model.

The manufacturers found two educators who became proficient articulators of this social efficiency philosophy: David Snedden and Charles Prosser. Snedden left a professorship at Teachers College to become Commissioner of Education in 1909 under Governor Douglas in Massachusetts. He appointed his colleague Prosser to create and administer the new vocational program. Snedden was a pioneer of educational sociology, the first editor of *The American Vocational Journal,* and according to Norman Woefel, among the "molders of the American mind." Prosser became Executive Secretary of the National Society for the Promotion of Industrial Education in 1912 and was the effective author of the Smith-Hughes Act. He became Director of the Dunwoody Institute of Vocational Training in Minneapolis and the first Executive Director of the Federal Board of Vocational Education.

The rationale Snedden and Prosser developed to support a technocratic training model was marked by a conservative social philosophy, a methodology of specific training based on principles of stimulus-response psychology, and a curriculum designed according to the job needs of industry.

The doctrine of social efficiency they espoused contained an image of man, a vision of the good society, and a set of related recommendations for school practice, not only for vocational education but for education in general as well.

Snedden confidently viewed the growth of the corporate-urban industrial complex as the foremost means for human progress. He called those who bemoaned the mechanization and depersonalization of work "simple-lifers" or "romantic impracticalists." Modern men might endure fragmented, routine job tasks; but production specialization and differentiation helped them live longer and more comfortably, and with leisure enough to consume the arts. Moreover, the application of mass production methods to "school life" could bring still more advances. As Snedden put it, "Quantity production methods applied in education speedily give us school grades, uniform textbooks, promotional examinations . . . strictly scheduled programs, mechanical discipline, and hundreds of other mechanisms most of which are unavoidably necessary if our ideals of universal education are to be realized."[4]

Snedden furthermore was convinced that the new science of sociology showed that characteristics of the population fitted neatly the needs of the corporate economy. He quoted his sociology teacher Franklin Giddings: "The process of selection is based upon the differences growing out of the unequal conditions of both heredity and nurture to which man is born. Inequality—physical, mental, and moral—is an inevitable characteristic of the social population."[5]

Snedden likened the good society to a winning team made stronger by the specialization of functions. Some, like the officers on a submarine crew, would be trained to lead and coordinate; others would be trained for their special functions in the ranks.[6]

As Snedden saw it, scientific testing instruments combined with vocational guidance would make it possible for schools to do what Charles Eliot had suggested in 1907—differentiate children into programs according to their "probable destinies" based on heredity plus economic and social factors. The new junior high schools would perform the task of sorting students into differentiated courses with pre-vocational offerings in commercial subjects, industrial arts, and agricultural or household arts for those "who most incline to them or have need of them."

Seen properly the condition of inequality was not something to be deplored but a fact which would help us all more toward a common goal. Men of industry and labor might have their conflicts, but they were in agreement about the proper motivation and goal of progress. Samuel Gompers, after all, was willing to boil down the goal of his wing of the labor movement to that single potent word—"More." Snedden shared that sentiment and felt that new insights into the rationalization of labor could now be applied to schooling in ways that would enable all Americans, at all levels, to advance in the common quest for More. It was a clear example of what Green tells us has been a basic expectation of Americans—the function of the schools is to help you get ahead in the system.

The model that emerged from this motivation was a social Darwinist "job efficiency" approach. The nature of the jobs to be planned for school children would roughly parallel the design of jobs in the work world. Application of the rationalization of labor could increase the efficiency and productivity in both realms. The question of whether or not such arrangements were instrumental in helping children "find a work" (in Green's sense) could be dismissed as the talk one might expect from "easy-lifers."

The job efficiency approach was projected as the proper model for the whole school effort. This appears in Snedden's way of defining the relation of vocational and liberal studies. As he saw it, "Man stands to the world about him in a two-fold relationship. He is a producer of utilites . . . and he must utilize utilities."[7] The education that trains him to be a good producer is vocational education. The education that trains him to be a good utilizer or consumer is liberal education.

The job efficiency approach seems to have genuine relevance for aspects of vocational skill training, and Charles Prosser, the father of the Smith-Hughes Act, was a creative pioneer in these efforts. His passion for specificity of training, however, kept his version of vocational education from attaining the flexibility required to meet rapid technical and social change. The program Prosser developed at Dunwoody mirrored the approach he and Snedden favored. They wanted "real vocational education" not some pseudo-manual type of training. This meant creating courses that taught the skills and techniques of specific callings. For its goals, vocational education should go (they said) "consistently to the world of economic activity." Short unit courses were programmed in great detail to lead students through the skill development cycle. Students punched in on time clocks and instructors acted like shop foremen. If students were not punctual, orderly, and efficient, they were asked to leave.

The danger in the job efficiency-social control model occurs when zealous proponents commit the reductionist fallacy of proposing it as the prototype for all of education. One example may illustrate the point.

Snedden clarified his new proposals for liberal studies in an address to the New England History Teachers' Association in 1914. He characterized the old chronological approach to history as "cold storage" education and said that for "the rank and file" history could be taught to "satisfy specific aims drawn from functional social needs." History was for citizenship. "Having once conceived of the citizen as we should like to have him, we can work back and by analysis find the numberless specific forms of training by which we can produce this type." On the question of which social values the teacher should advocate, Snedden said the teacher should remember that he was a public servant with an obligation to teach "the opinions and valuations of the controlling majority." A teacher interested in minority views should either surrender them to majority opinion or leave.[8]

When the United States Commissioner of Education Philander P. Claxton admitted to "a shudder of abhorrence" at the "brutal efficiency" implied by this new and more effective education, Snedden replied that he, too, stood for cultural education. But the proper definition of both cultural and vocational education had to be derived from an analysis of the social functions each should perform. These functions were to be revealed by insights from educational sociology, a new discipline of which Snedden was the foremost practitioner.

Snedden based his concept of society and schooling on a job efficiency model. The task of schooling was "to make the child a better socius," a fitter member of an efficiently functioning society. The school in both its vocational and liberal aspects should be modeled on the "job" as archetype. Schooling should sort us out according to our various capacities. As we all become more efficient in the slots right for us, we enlarge the pie we have to consume.

The school tasks we perform for our teachers may not engage our personal selves. But who needs it? If schooling does its job—provides access to higher income—then we can find personal sustenance elsewhere—in our private lives, families, churches, and fraternal organizations. Meanwhile, we can learn in school how to cope with or con the system.

John Dewey and the Policy Issues of Vocationalism

In that other wing of progressivism, John Dewey was seriously involved with the policy issues connected with vocationalism. But Dewey, the philosopher of democracy, brought a different frame of reference to bear on the topic. Two brief quotations provide a feeling for the value orientation he spoke from: "The dominant vocation of all human beings at all times is living—intellectual and moral growth."[9] And he said in *Reconstruction in Philosophy:*

> All social institutions have a meaning, a purpose. That purpose is to set free and to develop the capacities of human individuals without respect to race, sex, class or economic status. . . . [The] test of their value is the extent to which they educate every individual into the full stature of his possibility. Democracy has many meanings, but if it has a moral meaning, it is found in resolving that the supreme test of all political institutions and industrial arrangement shall be the contribution they make to the all-around growth of every member of society.[10]

To Snedden this kind of talk sounded like the "romantic impracticalists," and he confessed to a difficulty in understanding Dewey's position. He was hurt when he found Dewey opposing the German dualism, and in a letter to *The New Republic,* he said, "to find Dr. Dewey apparently giving aid and comfort to the opponents of a broader, richer, and more effective program of education . . . is discouraging." Dewey replied sharply that his differences with Snedden were profoundly social and political as well as educational.

> The kind of vocational education in which I am interested is not one which will "adapt" workers to the existing industrial regime; I am not sufficiently in love with the regime for that. It seems to me that the business of all who would not be educational timeservers is to resist every move in this direction, and to strive for a kind of vocational education which will first alter the existing industrial system, and ultimately transform it.[11]

The differences were indeed profoundly social and political. Dewey's primary loyalty was to democracy as a way of living and working. Rather than putting vocationalism unquestioningly at the service of corporate industrial needs, Dewey's aspiration was to redesign industrial and educational institutions so that they would support democratic values. An incident in 1915 suggested that he was not alone with his progressivism.

At a joint meeting of the National Vocational Guidance Association (NVGA) and the National Society for the Promotion of Industrial Education (NSPIE), with Charles Prosser as the latter's Executive Secretary, a group of "progressives" led the NVGA into refusing Prosser's invitation to join his organization. The "humanitarians" were represented by speakers like Ida Tarbell, queen of the muckrakers, arguing for the inclusion of girls in industrial education; Owen R. Lovejoy, Secretary of the National Child Labor Committee; and representatives of a Chicago reform group (notably George H. Mead and

Frank Leavitt of the University of Chicago) who joined John Dewey in opposing pressures to establish separate vocational schools.

Owen R. Lovejoy enunciated the point of view represented by this wing. He told the convention that both industries and schools needed to be reformed before children could experience the "promise of America." The schools, he said, should introduce programs of vocational guidance which would "analyze our industries and train our youth to distinguish between a 'vocation' and a 'job.' " He criticized the "captains of industry" who said, "Here are the jobs: What kind of children have you to offer?" Educators and guidance personnel, he said, must reverse the inquiry and say, "Here are your children: What kind of industry have you to offer?"[12]

Frank Leavitt, who was to become the first President of the NVGA, supported Lovejoy's position. He said guidance workers needed to study industries from the point of view of whether they were "good for children." Such studies, "if carried out in a comprehensive, purposeful, scientific way, may force upon industry many modifications which will be good not only for the children but for industry as well." Vocational guidance will not hesitate to make such demands just because an industry is rich and powerful, Leavitt added. "Why should we hesitate to lay hands on industry in the name of education when we have already laid hands on the school in the name of industry."[13]

While attending the 1913 convention, John Dewey was at work on the thoughts that would emerge in *Democracy and Education*. In that 1916 book, Dewey said that "the chief issue" in the conflict of philosophical theories was focusing on "discussion of the proper place and function of vocational factors in education."[14] It is worth noting that his most famous chapter on the vocational issue was not entitled "Vocational Education" but "Vocational Aspects in Education."

Eager to advocate vocational aspects in education as a pivotal instrument of school reform, Dewey encountered a major frustration in distinguishing his point of view from the version of vocational education advanced by Snedden and Prosser.

Dewey's central concern was with the problem of people and of democratic traditions in the technological society. He rejected the image of isolated individuals moved by the play of natural forces in the marketplace. He operated from the social psychology position of his colleague George H. Mead—with its "self-other" concept of personality: the self as emerging from both the pattern of culture and the value choices of the individual. The premise held that if you wanted people with the qualities capable of sustaining democratic values, they had to be nourished in communities marked by such values. As Dewey saw it, people had begun to mouth the rhetoric of democratic values while living in daily contradiction of them.

The task of overcoming the contradictions, as Dewey defined it, was to develop strategies for bringing qualities of the democratic ethos into institutions being transformed by science, technology, and corporation. His general strategy was to seek means by which the qualities of mind required to reform institutions could be made available across the entire population.

In his design, the schools were assigned a critical role: they could teach the habits of thinking hypothetically; of testing conjectures against experience; of freely exchanging conclusions; and of tolerating maverick ideas and lifestyles. The schools could be turned into collaborative learning communities where the young in living and learning would experience the life qualities exemplified in the creative work places of scientists, artists, and craftsmen. By spending the years of childhood and youth in such learning communities, children might become the kind of people who could make institutional styles liberating rather than manipulative.

In *Democracy and Education,* Dewey struggled to explain his argument about how "vocational aspects" or "occupations" could become major instruments for general school reform:

> Both practically and philosophically the key to the present educational situation lies in a gradual reconstruction of school materials and methods so as to utilize various forms of occupations typifying social callings, and to bring out their intellectual and moral content. . . . This educational reorganization cannot be accomplished by merely trying to give a technical preparation for industries and professions as they now operate, much less by merely reproducing industrial conditions in the school. The problem is not that of making the schools an adjunct to manufacture and commerce, but of utilizing the factors of industry to make school life more active, more full of immediate meaning, more connected with out-of-school experience. The problem is not easy of solution. There is a standing danger that education will perpetuate the older traditions for a select few, and effect its adjustment to the new economic conditions more or less on the basis of acquiescence in the untransformed, unrationalized, and unsocialized phases of our defective industrial regime.[15]

The key recommendation is to use occupations in a way "to bring out their intellectual and moral content" for both students and workers.

The complexity of Dewey's position is indicated in the tortuous analysis he made of such related terms as "occupation," "vocations," and "callings." On the one hand, Dewey spoke of "occupations" as forms of work available in the new industrial era, and he described how work in industry and commerce was being transformed by scientific and technological factors.

> Industry has ceased to be essentially an empirical rule of thumb procedure, handed down by custom. Its technique is now technological: that is to say based upon machinery resulting from discoveries in mathematics, physics, chemistry, bacteriology, etc. . . . While the intellectual possibilities of industry have multiplied, industrial conditions tend to make industry, for the great masses, less of an educative resource than it was in the days of hand production for local markets. The burden of realizing the intellectual possibilities inhering in work is thus thrown back on the school.[16]

In practice, however, said Dewey, the schools were not seizing opportunities to draw on the intellectual possibilities of industry. Premature training for salable skills neglected the liberalizing dimension of exploring things in terms of their broader meanings and of raising questions about human values. Public school trade training, because of its sharp focus on job skills, tended to create members of a permanent, subordinate working class. If denied access to liberalizing experiences, workers would not be prepared to help transform an unsatisfying industrialism into something more civilized.

In that same chapter, however, Dewey also used the terms "occupation" or "vocation" in ways which had nothing to do with earning a living. We must avoid, he said, using vocation or occupation to apply only to activities where tangible commodities are produced, or to imply that each person has only one vocation. In its broader definition, an occupation "is a continuous activity having a purpose." In this sense, it is something with which an individual is occupied; it is something in which he is interested and to which he is committed. Each individual, in this sense, has a variety of "occupations," "callings," or "vocations." He may earn his living as a garment worker or an engineer. But he may also be active in community affairs, or he may be passionately committed to playing the oboe. We tend, Dewey said, to name a person's vocation according to his employment. "But we should not allow ourselves to be so subject to works as to ignore and virtually deny his other callings when it comes to the vocational phases of education."

His general point was that one's vocation, both in the sense of one's work and of one's central concerns, plays a critical role in self-fulfillment and continuing education.

> A calling is also of necessity an organizing principle for information and ideas; for knowledge and intellectual growth. It provides an axis which runs through an immense diversity of detail; it causes different experiences, facts, items of information to fall into order one with another. The lawyer, the physician, the laboratory investigator in some branch of chemistry, the parent, the citizen interested in his own locality, has a constant working stimulus to note and relate whatever has to do with his concern or his occupation. He unconsciously, from the motivation of his occupation, reaches out for all relevant information, and holds to it.[17]

In this sense the schools had an important function in helping people find their vocations or their work; although in a genuinely humane community, all the other institutions would have that function too.

The critical question Dewey asked in *Individualism Old and New* is: "Can a material, industrial civilization be converted into a distinct agency for liberating the minds and refining the emotions of all who take part in it?" Such a "humanism," he said, "will have to face the question of whether work itself can become an instrument of culture and of how the masses can share freely in a life enriched in imagination and aesthetic enjoyment. This task is set not because of sentimental 'humanitarianism,' but [because] of the intellectual conviction that while men belong in nature and mind is connected with matter, humanity and its collective intelligence are the means by which nature is guided to new possibilities."[18]

When Dewey was at the University of Chicago he created the elementary Laboratory School where he put his ideas to work. He conceived it as a small collaborative learning-work community. Studies were organized around such "occupations" as weaving, gardening, cooking, and constructing. Studies in the sciences, history, language, mathematics, and the arts were related to these activities. Children, for example, could get the feeling of how science and technology had affected such a basic process as the turning of raw wool into clothing, by first trying the process by hand and then observing factory methods. They could also study what the social and human effects were when men moved from handicraft to corporate industrial modes of production. As students grew older, activities and studies could be extended to the out-of-school community.

Dewey deliberately designed his school as a small learning community in order to preserve collaborative working relations. When William Rainey Harper, President of the University of Chicago, put pressure on Dewey to expand enrollments to increase revenue, Dewey resisted because expansion "would involve such a complete change in the ideals and methods of the school as profoundly to modify its whole character."[19] In other words, Dewey sensed the need for smallness within large organizations.[20] In his image of new kinds of schools, or schools within schools, which would have the marks of learning-work communities, Dewey definitely saw an alternative to the Snedden-Prosser job efficiency model. In the article he called "Learning to Earn" Dewey said,

> Instead of trying to split schools into two kinds, one of a trade type for children whom it is assumed are to be employees and one of a liberal type for the children of the well-to-do, it will aim at such a reorganization of existing schools as will give all pupils a genuine respect for useful work, an ability to render service, and a contempt for social parasites whether they are called tramps or leaders of "society." . . . It will indeed make much of developing motor and manual skill, but not of a routine or automatic type. It will rather utilize active and manual pursuits as the means of developing constructive, inventive and creative powers of mind. It will select the materials and the technique of the trades not for the sake of producing skilled workers for hire in definite trades, but for the sake of securing industrial intelligence—a knowledge of the conditions and processes of present manufacturing, transportation and commerce so that the individual may be able to make his own choices and his own adjustments, and be master, so far as in him lies, of his own economic fate. It will be recognized that, for this purpose, a broad acquaintance with science and skill in the laboratory control of materials and processes is more important than skill in trade operations. It will remember that the future employee is a consumer as well as a producer, that the whole tendency of society, so far as it is intelligent and wholesome, is to an increase of the hours of leisure, and that an education which does nothing to enable individuals to consume wisely and to utilize leisure wisely is a fraud on democracy. So far as method is concerned, such a conception of industrial education will prize freedom more than docility; initiative more than automatic skill; insight and understanding more than capacity to recite lessons or to execute tasks under the direction of others.[21]

Conclusion

We can recognize ourselves in the images of both the Dewey and the Snedden-Prosser philosophies. They reflect our divided soul—the two yearnings, for social efficiency on the one hand, and sanity through community and fulfillment in work on the other.

We have not yet been all one or the other. But we have a tendency, under duress, to opt for "More" and for job efficiency, often at the expense of our sanity. (We may be spending as much as $240 million a year for armed and unarmed school guards to maintain an essentially job-oriented approach to schooling.)[22]

As we seek to reduce discontent and alienation among a more highly educated population, we may have to redesign both schools and industries so that they have more of the qualities of collaborative work-learning places. We just might, at that time, address ourselves to the question suggested by Lynn White, Jr., in *The Dynamo and the Virgin Reconsidered:* how to build a "high democratic civilization" under technology.[23] I think both Dewey and Green directed their thinking toward this important question.

Notes

1. Arthur G. Wirth, *Education in the Technological Society: The Vocational-Liberal Studies Controversy in the Early Twentieth Century.* New York: Intext, now Thomas Y. Crowell, 1972. Some passages in this discussion originally appeared in "Historical and Social Context of Career Education," *Journal of Career Education* 2 (Fall 1975): 2.
2. Thomas F. Green, *Work, Leisure and the American Schools.* New York: Random House, 1968, p. 44.
3. Ibid., p. 37.
4. David Snedden, *Toward Better Educations.* New York: Bureau of Publications, Teachers College, Columbia University, 1931, pp. 330–31.
5. Franklin Giddings, *Principles of Sociology.* New York: Macmillan, 1896, p. 9.
6. David Snedden, "Education for a World of Teamplayers and Teamworkers," *School and Society* 20 (1 Nov. 1924): 554.
7. David Snedden, "Fundamental Distinctions Between Liberal and Vocational Education," N.E.A. *Proceedings,* 1914, pp. 154–55.
8. David Snedden, "Teaching History in Secondary Schools," *History Teachers Magazine* 5 (Nov. 1914): 277–82; and "Liberty of Teaching in the Social Sciences," *School and Society* 13 (12 Feb. 1921): 185–86.
9. John Dewey, *Democracy and Education.* New York: Macmillan, 1916, p. 362.
10. John Dewey, *Reconstruction in Philosophy.* New York: New American Library (Mentor Books), 1950, p. 147.
11. *The New Republic* 3 (15 May 1915): 40, 42.
12. Owen R. Lovejoy, "Vocational Guidance and Child Labor," U.S. Bureau of Education *Bulletin,* No. 14. Washington: U.S. Government Printing Office, 1914, p. 13.

13. Frank M. Leavitt, "How Shall We Study the Industries for the Purposes of Vocational Guidance," U.S. Bureau of Education *Bulletin*, No. 14. Washington: U.S. Government Printing Office, 1914, pp. 79–81.

14. Dewey, *Democracy and Education*, p. 358.

15. Ibid., pp. 369–70.

16. Ibid., p. 367.

17. Ibid., p. 362.

18. John Dewey, *Individualism Old and New*. New York: Capricorn, 1962 (original, 1929), pp. 124–26.

19. John Dewey, "Letters to William Rainey Harper," *The President's Papers*. University of Chicago (23 June 1898).

20. In this sense his ideas are congruent with the thinking of the contemporary social philosopher E.F. Schumacher in *Small Is Beautiful: Economics As If Peopled Mattered*. New York: Harper and Row, 1973.

21. John Dewey, "Learning to Earn," *Education Today*. New York: G. P. Putnam and Sons, 1940, pp. 131–32.

22. *Phi Delta Kappan,* December 1974, p. 254.

23. Lynn White, Jr., *The Dynamo and the Virgin Reconsidered*. Cambridge: M.I.T. Press, 1971.

Educational Relevance
for Future Employer
or Future Employee?

PAUL C. GILMORE

Professional and technical education is supposed to be relevant: relevant to the job the student eventually fills, to the needs of society, and to the needs of the student himself. But conflicts appear between the needs of the future employer and those of the future employee, and appropriate roles can be assigned to the different agencies only when these needs are understood.

A university professor recently asked the data processing manager of a large corporation to list the main deficiencies he found in the educations of the people he hired. He replied that they were often able to program in the exotic languages favored by their colleges but could use COBAL, the most widely applicable commercial language, only after weeks of training. The professor replied that the objective of his university was not to train COBAL programmers but rather to educate people who would, thereafter, grow on the educational base they had received.

The manager's complaint is real: the people he hires must begin at the beginning with narrow tasks requiring specific skills. He cannot use graduates who do not have those specific skills. But the professor, too, has a point: the long-term benefits of education should not be sacrificed to the narrow training required by employers.

The conflict between the short-term skill requirements of employers and the long-term educational needs of the employees can be lessened (I will suggest a mechanism later) but cannot be completely resolved. Yet if one recognizes that the long-term needs of employer and employee frequently coincide, much of the conflict becomes moot.

Most American corporations seek employment stability. They try to attract those people with potential for long-term growth, and they offer those people benefits that increase with the length of employment. The picture of a business ready to hire and fire according to last month's sales is more fiction than reality. Barring flagrant dishonesty, laziness, or personality disintegration, the employees of most American corporations can expect lifelong employment with major job changes occurring only as a result of their own desires. Consequently, given the choice between hiring someone with the narrow technical skills for today's job and someone with a broad education on which many different skills can be based, most businesses would choose the latter. In fact, most businesses are used to training their personnel for a wide range of specific tasks and often make this investment many times in an employee's career.

The data processing manager mentioned earlier voiced a second complaint about the programmers and analysts he hires—a complaint heard many times in different contexts. He said that even some of his best people find it difficult to document the programs they write in clear technical prose.

The professor recognized here a failing in his area. Moreover, writing skill is a base upon which many different jobs depend, and it is a skill adaptable to many tasks. Yet good technical writing rests upon general writing principles that can and should be taught and practiced before the specialized technical knowledge is acquired.

The ability to write clear prose is an example of a traditional goal of education—providing a long-range benefit for both employer and employee. It is a broad skill that cannot be readily acquired on the job, yet it is often overlooked in technical education.* Good writing usually reflects clear thinking—another traditional goal of education, and one few people would dispute. That goal, like other traditional goals, confers benefits on those who achieve it well beyond those accruing from the work environment.

One often hears that an important goal of modern education is to prepare people for the increasing leisure time that will be theirs to enjoy during the working years and after retirement. That leisure time has not, however, appeared in the abundance we all expected, and when it does appear, it is often consumed by second jobs. People

---

*Even those with little knowledge of computer programming will appreciate the need Frederick P. Brooks, Jr., expresses for precise prose in his book *The Mythical Man-Month* (1975). See especially his sixth chapter, "Passing the Word."

take these second jobs sometimes, but not always, for economic reasons. People often like to feel useful to society; and they want to receive recognition, not just money, for their usefulness. (How else can one explain the vast army of volunteers that keeps America's cultural and charitable and political organizations thriving?) Thus an essential responsibility of education is to prepare one for a civic life that is often work-oriented in the sense that it demands the same skills and abilities as work.

There is nothing wrong with the idea that a primary function of education is the bettering of one's employment opportunities, as long as it is understood that the opportunities are for a more satisfying life and not necessarily a wealthier life. The educational system should prepare an individual for a lifetime of jobs, some paid, some voluntary, some part-time, and some full-time, for through these jobs an individual gives shape and meaning to his life and derives important satisfactions.

Professor Thomas Green also emphasizes the traditional goals of education: to prepare a student for a wide range of contributions in civic life as well as in business life; and to provide the general skills, not specialized training, that give a student a wider sense of self and world so that with initiative the student can shape a life of satisfying work and learning. Professor Green's point that the quality of an education is of greater importance than its mere attainment cannot be overemphasized.*

It is time to ask how that data processing manager is to obtain employees who can write COBAL programs when traditional education does not produce COBAL programmers. Or more generally, what can be done to lessen the conflict between the short-term needs of the employer and the long-term needs of the student? The question can be answered, I believe, by narrowing the gap between the largely individual effort of education and the considerably greater cooperative effort of work. Narrowing this gap might, at the same time, help students prepare themselves for the short-term needs of their future employers.

My devotion to the traditional goals of education does not imply an equal devotion to traditional methods of teaching. Modern tech-

---

*That it has been lost sight of is evident from the article "Rise in Remedial Work Taxing Colleges" by Gene I. Maeroff in *The New York Times,* 7 March 1976, p. 7.

nological developments, like Xerography, permit different instructional methods—and the costs of education demand them. Some modern methods of teaching rely on individual discipline and motivation, qualities distributed unequally among students. I would like to suggest an experimental style of class organization that exploits this unequal distribution in a way somewhat similar to the way it is exploited in the organization of work.

Everyone has heard of team teaching—several teachers, each bringing his own special assets and defects to class in a cooperative teaching effort. And everyone has heard of individual learning, where a student is responsible for covering the material of a course at his own pace and under his own direction, possibly with the help of a teacher. Why not, then, "team learning," where eight or ten students become jointly responsible for covering the material of a course at their own pace, under their own direction, and possibly with the help of a teacher? The team should comprise students of mixed abilities, bringing a balance of discipline, intelligence, and motivation to the team. In the cooperative learning effort, each member of the team would have to make a contribution. Consequently the team would be responsible for judging the capacities and contributions of each of its members—not, however, for judging their final knowledge of the course material.

Since the learning pace would be established by the team, the preparation of materials and the testing of knowledge would be done in much the same way as for individual learning. And computer management or assistance could be used where appropriate.

The benefits of team learning might include both the mastery of specific material and skills (COBAL programming, if you like) and experience with cooperative striving toward common goals. Students would learn how to work with people of different abilities; how to give assistance and direction to those of lesser abilities; and how to take assistance and direction from those with greater abilities. These are, of course, all valuable skills.

Team learning might also help schools overcome one obstacle to providing training in specific skills—namely, the difficulty of finding and the expense of keeping a faculty able to teach the specific skills demanded in areas undergoing rapid technological change.

The world of business is filled with potential teachers without, however, the time and energy to devote to the traditional teaching methods. While they might resist having to organize lecture notes, some of them could be lured into cooperative efforts. They could help faculty members gather material and prepare tests. And they could meet regularly with learning teams to field the questions the teams cannot answer on their own. In courses organized this way, one teacher could oversee many more classes than he would otherwise be able to. Teachers would, of course, have to accept the possibility of their knowledge of the material being somewhat less than that of the course graduates. And the teacher-scholar image might be replaced by a teacher-organizer image. But the gains might be worth it.

Nothing can entirely bridge the gap between school and work. The gap exists to provide a future employee with an education that yields long-term benefits for both him and his employer. But the managers of the world of work will forever be complaining of the lack of specific skills in the people they hire, and teachers will, I hope, forever be pointing out to them their shortsightedness. Nevertheless, attempts should be made to lessen the gap. Team learning might help to satisfy simultaneously both the short-term and the long-term needs of the students.

II
The Relationship
of Education
to Employment
and Work

Technological Unemployment and Occupational Education

LESTER C. THUROW

The ideal education-labor market information system is conventionally described as if it would function this way: Labor economists would make detailed projections of the skills that the economy will demand over the next five to ten years. These skill demands would be based on the economic growth of the economy and its rate of technical change. Both are necessary since economic growth increases the aggregate demand for skills of all types while technical change alters the mix of skills to be used within any given level of output.

At the same time, manpower and educational specialists would be projecting the flow of labor skills that will come into the market given the current structure of labor training programs. The result would be a projected vector of labor skill supplies that could be compared with the vector of labor skill demands. By comparing the two vectors, it would be possible both to list and to quantify those skills where there will be shortages and surpluses over the ensuing decade.

Based on their knowledge of skill shortages and surpluses, those in vocational education would alter their mix of training programs. Training would be cut back in surplus areas and expanded in shortage areas. By altering the training mix, occupational education would bring the demands and supplies of laboring skills into equilibrium. In the process, a set of highly desirable outputs would occur: labor skill surpluses and the resulting unemployment would be eliminated; labor skill shortages would vanish; economic bottlenecks in the economy would be broken; economic output would rise; and price increases would moderate. Individuals would be given highly marketable skills and would escape unemployment.

Unfortunately there are several reasons why this ideal vocational education-labor market information system is inappropriate in the present economy. And to be useful both to individuals and to society, occupational education must realize that it exists in an economic environment where it cannot function as this model suggests it should.

A Fundamental Fact of Life

As of January 1976 almost 8.5 percent of the American labor force, approximately eight million workers, was unemployed. If you look at the 1976 *Economic Report of the President,* Gerald Ford did not expect unemployment to average 7 percent before 1977 or to reach 5 percent until the end of 1980.[1] In this economic climate, occupational education can yield no social benefits. The basic problem is not a shortage of skills but a surplus of skills of almost all types and a shortage of jobs of all types.

Technical progress will probably proceed at its normal rate over the next five years, but it is unlikely to generate the types of skill shortages that produce an economic role for formal occupational training. We currently have a surplus of almost all labor skills, and these surpluses are not projected to disappear until the 1980s under current economic policies. Technical change may produce a demand for entirely new skills that we have not yet envisioned, but these skills will have little impact on the labor force for the next decade. A new product or technique is only gradually introduced into the economy and does not exert an impact until it has been in existence for some time. Thus any skill that might employ a significant percentage of the labor force is already in existence. There may be limited demand for as yet unknown skills, but these will represent only a small fraction of new job entrants.

Short-run vacancies or shortages may, of course, occur; and firms may complain about the shortage of "high-quality" workers. Any dynamic economy will have brief shortages of this or that skill, even if it is grossly underemployed. Any shortages will, however, be eliminated by informal on-the-job retraining and labor mobility long before vocational education authorities gear up to meet the demand. Complaints about shortages and the lack of high-quality workers were heard even during the Great Depression when unemployment was 25 percent and the social programs that supposedly create lazy workers had yet to appear. Because of the ever-present desire for "better" workers, there will always be a market for those with backgrounds that indicate they are superior to other unemployed individuals. In this environment, occupational education may yield private benefits, if it can certify superiority; but its social benefits will be zero. Every person trained and employed will simply displace someone else. Training will raise neither employment nor output. It will merely reshuffle unemployment.

Those in occupational education often ask where labor shortages will exist over the next five years, and the only truthful answer is nowhere. Neither the normal growth of the economy nor changes in its technology will create skill demands that cannot be met out of the existing pool of skills or by informal on-the-job training. If one thinks of occupational education as a social program designed to increase economic growth and lower unemployment, he thinks of a role that the economy will suppress for at least the next half decade. If it were not for the difficulties and costs of stopping and starting educational programs, any short-run cost-benefit analysis of occupational education would show that it should be shut down over the next five years. It will be turning out products for which there is no net demand.

In an underemployed environment, all education is simply a certification process rather than a skill-creating process. One plays a zero sum game where the winner is not a person with some needed set of skills, but someone who has been certified as relatively superior to other perfectly competent job applicants. Occupational education will be privately successful (that is, will yield jobs and earnings) only to the extent that it is perceived as a source of superior workers.

To be socially useful, formal occupational education must exist in an economic environment where the basic problem is a shortage of skills. If this shortage is to exist, the economy must be at or close to full employment. Since the economy is not going to be near full employment for some period, occupational education will not be able to play the role it would undoubtedly like to play in the economy.

A Problem of Substitution

Given a full employment economy, one hears the lament that the trouble with vocational education lies in the failure of labor economists to project labor supplies and demands with the precision educational planners need. While economists certainly are not projecting labor supplies and demands accurately, the problem is not one of unwillingness or ignorance. Essentially the economist is asked to do something that cannot be done—any more than astronomers can alter the laws of heavenly motion.

If the ideal model is to be applicable, the economy would make it difficult to substitute one skill for another, or capital for labor, in the production process. In the jargon of economists, the elasticity of substitution between skills and between capital and labor would have to be low. Similarly on the supply side, it must be difficult, or at least time-consuming, to alter labor skills. If both supply and demand elasticities of substitution are small, shortages can be clearly identified and quantified.

If, however, elasticities of substitution are high, one skill can be easily substituted for another, capital can be easily substituted for labor, and workers can quickly alter their laboring skills on the job. In this case, vacancies and projected skill shortages lose their concreteness. There is no vector of skills or capital-labor combinations that the economy must have. It can operate with many distributions of skills. Vacancies and skill shortages occur, but they are quickly eliminated through labor substitutions, capital replacement, or on-the-job training rather than by vocational education programs.

The empirical magnitude of the relevant elasticities of substitution depend on the level of aggregation of occupational skills. At some levels of aggregation, the elasticities are low, and at others they are high. Generally, the more aggregate the vector of labor skills, the lower the elasticities of substitution between different skills. The elasticities of substitution between different types of electricians are much higher than those between craftsmen and professional workers. But even there they are quite high when capital substitutions are allowed.

Without a doubt, there is a conflict between the accuracy and detail of those skill projections economists are able to make and the accuracy and detail of labor projections vocational education planners desire. Just as good specific training programs require low elasticities of substitution, so do good labor projections. I am not a pessimist about the possibilities of making accurate labor projections, but if the elasticities of substitution are high, it is simply impossible to make them.

There is abundant evidence of high elasticities of substitution. Surveys indicate that most labor skills used in the economy can be learned quickly.[2] Evidence about the high mobility of workers and the frequency of job changes points in the same direction.[3] And if you ask firms whether they make internal projections of their future labor needs, you will find that most do not.[4] Why do so few firms bother to make detailed labor projections? Why are they so bad when they are made? Irrationality may be the answer, but I suspect that the elasticities of substitution in both supply and demand are so high that it makes no sense for private firms to attempt projections. Private skill projections cannot be found for the same reasons that economists are unable to make skill projections. High elasticities of substitution make them useless.

If neither labor economists nor private industry can make detailed skill projections, it makes little sense to attempt to organize an occupational education system that depends upon them. The system has to be organized to function usefully in a world where detailed labor supply and demand projections are unobtainable.

If accurate skill projections are impossible at the level of detail desired by vocational educators, then something may be wrong with the degree of specificity of the skills being taught in vocational education. The same factors that limit the detail possible in skill projections limit the specificity that *ought* to be built into vocational education.

The labor economist should make his projections as detailed as the elasticities of substitution allow, but vocational education cannot sensibly make its training any more detailed. To refuse to accept projections because they do not furnish the desired detail is simply to wish to plan for a world that does not exist. Thus the failure of the labor economist and private firms to make adequate projections for vocational education may imply more than simple sloth or ignorance.

The Source of Labor Skills

The conventional model of vocational education is based upon the neoclassic economic theory that the labor market exists to match labor demands with labor supplies. In the matching (or mismatching) process various signals appear. Businesses are told to raise wages and redesign jobs in sectors with skill shortages. Educational institutions are told to increase training programs. In surplus sectors, businesses are told to lower wages. Educational institutions reduce training programs. Young people are told to acquire skills in high-wage areas and are discouraged from acquiring skills offering low wages. In the process, each skill market is cleared with increases or reductions in wages in the short run and by a combination of wage changes, skill changes, and production process changes in the long run.

The key ingredient in this view of the world is the assumption that workers acquire laboring skills exogenously in formal education or training and then bring these skills into the labor market. Possessing skills, they bid for the jobs that use them. Unfortunately, the underlying assumption is incorrect. Workers do not bring fully developed job skills to the labor market. Most cognitive job skills, general or specific, are acquired either formally or informally on the job after a worker wins an entry job and locates the associated promotion ladder.

The evidence for this observation is everywhere. In the 1960s the President's Commission on Automation undertook extensive surveys on how workers learned the actual cognitive job skills they used. Only 40 percent of the respondents reported that they used skills acquired in formal training programs or in specialized education. Most of them had, in fact, acquired their skills in informal, on-the-job training. Even among college graduates, over two-thirds reported that they had acquired cognitive job skills through informal, on-the-job processes.[5]

Perhaps the most convincing evidence came from workers asked to list the form of training that had been most helpful in acquiring their current job skills. Only 12 percent listed formal training and specialized education. Moreover, some of this special training had been provided at the place of work and depended directly upon the worker having already been selected for the job in question.

These results have an obvious explanation. Since training and production are complementary projects, most job skills are taught best in conjunction with an actual job. Goods and services produced during training can be sold to reduce training costs. Only actual production generates the degree of realism necessary to polish production skills. It also guarantees that the worker will know everything he needs to know without learning lots of extraneous information. On-the-job training is, in short, the most practical kind of training.

As a result, the labor market is not where fully developed skills bid for jobs. Rather it is where supplies of trainable workers are matched with training opportunities that are, in turn, directly associated with the number of job openings that exist. Training opportunities occur only when a job opening creates the demand for the skills in question.[6]

This process also explains why elasticities of substitution are high. One of the big advantages of OJT is that it helps an employer gain some control over the elasticities of substitution in the vector of labor skills supplied as well as those demanded. By using OJT, he can create a pool of partially trained workers who can be easily upgraded when demand requires. Thus part of the advantage of OJT is that it *creates* high elasticities of substitution between labor skills.

One of the problems facing vocational education is the fact that many employers establish internal labor markets with limited ports of entry. Regardless of personal skills, there are only a few jobs at which an individual can actually start. Acquired skills cannot be used until the worker has enough seniority to be eligible for the job that matches his skills. In fact, the internal labor market is designed to maximize training from one individual to another. Skilled workers can informally train less skilled workers in the confidence that their training will not cut their wages or cost them their jobs.

If you think of internal labor markets as places where a significant fraction of all skills are created and where most job opportunities are distributed, the goal of occupational education is to get graduates into internal labor markets that offer significant career training opportunities. In terms of the dual labor market hypothesis, the aim is to get graduates into the primary labor market with its training opportunities and out of the secondary market with its lack of career training opportunities.

The Comparative Advantages of Occupational Education

If occupational education is to play a useful role in the economy, it must recognize the existence of internal labor markets and the importance of informal, on-the-job training in transmitting skills. Given this environment, what can occupational education provide that will benefit both its clients and society? The answer lies in the fact that employers are interested in obtaining employees who occasion low on-the-job training costs rather than completely trained workers. Although on-the-job training may be informal, it is still costly in that production slackens while the training occurs.

Instead of focusing on projected labor skill shortages, occupational education should focus on establishing a complementary relationship with on-the-job training and on the process of placing trainees in those internal labor markets that offer training and promotion opportunities. This focus will require occupational education to produce graduates who are superior workers in the sense of having lower training costs as they move up the occupational ladder.

To sort out the natural division of responsibility between formal occupational education and informal on-the-job training, one should think about the comparative advantages of each. It is unlikely that formal occupational training can provide polished production job skills as cheaply as informal on-the-job training. But formal education has two distinct areas of advantage. As far as employers are concerned, it is a cheap place to determine whether workers do or do not have certain work habits. It is almost impossible, for example, to test whether a person will heed his alarm clock. Attendance records are the only indicative tests. Given that bad work habits tend to drive out good work habits, employers are reluctant to use their own shops to weed out the employees with the bad habits. They want this disruption to occur somewhere else.

It may be fair or unfair to ask schools either to teach industrial discipline or to sort out those individuals who do and do not have it. But this sorting is, in fact, one of the main economic services the educational system can perform. To the extent that schools junk standards of industrial discipline or fail to keep performance records, they reduce their economic value to both the student and the employer. Their credentials, moreover, no longer serve to place students in the desired labor market.

The second advantage of formal education lies in the area of teaching skills that require long periods to learn or skills where teaching many students at the same time provides substantial economies of scale. These tend to be general learning skills—motor and intellectual—rather than specific job skills. MIT engineers, for example, are in great demand. But if you look at what they are taught, they could by no stretch of the imagination jump right into work without on-the-job training. They learn the background skills that make it possible to absorb whatever on-the-job training they encounter. There is also a set of social skills—the art of persuasion, the ability to meet and talk with strangers—that can have a large payoff in the economy but seems to require a long incubation period. All schools are and should be, to a certain extent, "charm schools." Charm is a work skill just as much as welding. While such skills may not be directly teachable, they nonetheless should be transmitted along with specific information.

The large and largely pessimistic literature on the impact of manpower training programs reveals an increasing focus on the problems of motivation and industrial discipline rather than on the transmission of cognitive job skills.[7] Study after study indicates that the cognitive job skills are relatively easy to teach but that motivation and industrial discipline are virtually impossible to teach.

Emphasizing the value of general learning skills and good work habits does not slight the importance of specific cognitive job skills in the educational process. The best way to teach motivation, industrial discipline, general literacy, and trainability may be in the transmission of very specific cognitive job skills. The cognitive job skills may never be used, but they can serve as the vehicle around which these other skills are taught. Without learning specific job skills, students may not sit still long enough to learn the skills that have the long-run payoff.

Conclusion

From the point of view of occupational education, this discussion does not provide what its title implicitly promises, some analysis and estimation of the skill gaps that will be created by technical change. But even in the best of economic times, rigid skill gaps do not appear in the way the title implies. In the actual economic environment of the next five years, skill gaps will be caused neither by general economic growth nor by technical change. Unemployment rates will be so high that surpluses in almost all laboring skills will exist. Any skill shortages that do emerge will be eliminated by labor mobility or informal upgrading so quickly that occupational education will not be able to meet the perceived demand.

In this environment, jobs will be acquired for the graduates of occupational education not by inculcating unique labor skills (many workers will share these skills) but by being able to prove that graduates possess an inherently lower training cost than the other applicants. Thus occupational education must be in a position to certify that its graduates possess industrial discipline, "charm," and general learning skills and that they can be trained inexpensively.

Notes

1.   Council of Economic Advisors. *Economic Report of the President, 1976*. Washington: U.S. Government Printing Office, 1976.

2.   U.S. Department of Labor. *Formal Occupational Training of Adult Workers*. Washington: Manpower Automation Research Monograph 2, 1964.

3.   U.S. Department of Labor. *Employment and Earnings: Manpower Report of the President*. Washington: U.S. Government Printing Office, 1976.

4.   Gerald G. Somers, "The Response of Vocational Education to Labor Market Change," *Journal of Human Resources* 3 (1968): 47.

5.   U.S. Department of Labor. *Formal Occupational Training of Adult Workers.* Washington: Manpower Automation Research Monograph 2, 1964, pp. 3, 18, 20, 43.

6.   Lester C. Thurow, *Generating Inequality.* New York: Basic Books, 1975, chapters 4 and 5.

7.   See Michael K. Taussig, "An Economic Analysis of Vocational Education in the New York City Schools," or Arthur J. Corazzini, "The Decision to Invest in Vocational Education: An Analysis of Costs and Benefits," *Journal of Human Resources* 3 (1968).

An Alternative View
of Technological Unemployment
and Occupational Education

EDWIN L. HERR

Manpower forecasting, like meteorology, is less than an exact science, and its error variance is likely to be especially large when both individual and occupational characteristics are in dynamic flux—as they are now. But manpower forecasting, unlike weather prediction, is influenced by economic, political, and social shifts in values and directions. These, in turn, affect such matters as the types of goods and services people seek, the amounts of discretionary income available for such things as recreation and education, the images of what goals people value, and the types of educational emphases necessary to support the dynamics of the occupational structure. The transnational character of much of America's business and industry makes manpower forecasting vulnerable not only to shifts within our national boundaries but also to shifts stimulated by the OPEC nations, the Common Market countries, and other nations that affect the strategic interests of the United States. In point of fact, hardly any information is more difficult to obtain than accurate knowledge of present and future job opportunities.

Nevertheless, manpower forecasting is used in our democratic society, particularly in relation to educational planning. However, some people assume that the use of manpower forecasts as basic to the charting of the allocations of educational resources will lead ultimately to a limitation upon an individual's career choices and the educational pathway he follows to prepare for the career. Thus, while in an era of sparse resources educational planners cannot ignore manpower information, it may be seen as at least a potential deterrent to individual free choice. Manpower information can be, therefore, only one input of many into vocational education planning.

Next we face the fact, with Professor Lester Thurow, that the ideal vocational education-labor market information system—meshing labor skill demands with labor skills coming into the market via train-ing routes—is, given current realities, inappropriate. I am not sure that the system Professor Thurow describes would be ideal in this nation under the existing economic conditions or any others. In particular, the assumption of this system is that the unemployed are those whose skills are insufficient for employers to hire them at the prevailing wages. Unfortunately, this assumption overstates the de-sire of all people to accept whatever work is available and thus does not account for other sources of variance in employability (informa-tion and motivation, for example).

Such a model carries forth the Keynesian notion that people choose work that maximizes gain and minimizes monetary loss. It does not account for the potential of work to meet human relations, prestige, status, and other needs more important to many people than money alone. Nor does this model account for such governmental interven-tion as welfare, food stamps, and unemployment compensation, which provide many people with a base—indeed sometimes an incen-tive—to survive without working. Finally, human capital theories often fail to pay sufficient attention to such matters as the role of occupational information and social encouragement in motivating people to work. For these reasons alone, a model for vocational edu-cation planning that rests exclusively on matching and manipulating labor skill demands with labor skills produced is inadequate.

A Fundamental Fact of Life

According to the discussion which Professor Thurow calls "A Funda-mental Fact of Life," as of January 1976 almost 8.5 percent of the American labor force was unemployed. Moreover, he says, unem-ployment may not average 7 percent until 1977 and may not reach 5 percent until the end of 1980. Therefore, he concludes, occupa-tional education can yield few social benefits. I do not agree, and I consider it useful to put these unemployment figures into historical perspective.

Since World War II, unemployment rates exceeded 4 percent in at least 19 years, and in 11 of those years it surpassed 5 percent. Indeed, the United States entered the 1960s in a climate of unemployment. Unemployment in the third post-Korean War recession exceeded 8.1 percent (unadjusted for seasonality in February 1961) as compared with 7.6 percent in February 1976.[1] When President Kennedy took office in January of 1961, he apparently considered poverty and high unemployment the most serious problems facing the nation. He quickly appointed a panel of consultants on vocational education and began to initiate the series of laws that came to be called "antipoverty" in that they focused on the severe socioeconomic problems of large segments of the population: the Area Redevelopment Act, the Manpower Development and Training Act, the Economic Opportunity Act, and the Vocational Education Act of 1963.

There was intensive debate then, as there is now, about whether the cause of unemployment was slow economic growth and a deficient rate of job creation or inadequate skills in an economy of abundant but high-level employment opportunities.[2] We opted for the latter explanation and escalated vocational education opportunities, particularly for the hard-core unemployed, the disadvantaged, and people displaced by automation. In a number of ways, this skill training provided reentry to the labor force and a new start for many of its recipients. But it became clear early in the 1960s that focusing on occupational task skills alone was too limited a response. Thus remedial basic education, diagnosis of learning difficulties, self-concept development, decision-making skills, job search and interview skills, and work adjustment behaviors became part of the agenda of many programs during that period. In the course of these changes, the funding for much of vocational education—the Vocational Education Act of 1963 and the VEA amendments of 1968—began to reset the gyroscopes and priorities for this activity.

The primary concern under the Smith-Hughes Act and the successors to the 1963 legislation was to meet the skill needs of the labor market in a series of specific occupations. The 1963 Act reversed the priorities. The employability needs of the trainees were the primary concern, and training could occur in any recognized occupation. This shift did not relieve occupational education of its obligation to meet the skill needs of the labor market in those occupations where classroom and lab training might be the most efficient methods of skill development. Rather, it became obvious that either attaining personal competence as a worker or meeting the skill needs of the labor market required more than excellent occupational task skills alone. Longitudinal processes of self-identity and career identity; awareness of opportunities; personal feelings of competence, choice, and value commitments—among other emphases in pre-vocational activity—were seen as highly important to occupational task acquisition. Many of these emphases had to be attained through new relationships between general and vocational education, as well as through the total educational enterprise and the larger community.

In a sense, this situation still exists as the nation develops and implements models of career education comprised, in part, of vocational or occupational education.

I do not agree with Professor Thurow that occupational education can yield few social benefits. He sees the basic problem not as a shortage of skills but as a surplus of skills of almost all types and a shortage of jobs of all types. If one looks at the matter in national quantitative terms, that may be true. But several factors must also be considered.

First, for the near future a "bumping down" phenomenon will operate in many occupations. The master's degree holder will do what baccalaureate people formerly did; baccalaureates will take the places of associate degree people; and so on down the range of educational credentials. Thus we will find underemployment rather than unemployment. Underemployment is obviously a problem in its own right since people who are overeducated for their work experience status conflict and feelings of alienation. The problem becomes acute in a society where the labor force is highly educated.

Second, the United States may well have a supply of jobs between now and 1985, but those jobs may change their characteristics. Accordng to O'Toole, for example, the demand for qualified workers in the lower level jobs will soon exceed the supply.[3] At the same time, the supply of highly qualified workers will exceed demand in higher level jobs. But no "shortages" or "surpluses" will occur at either end of the spectrum since the labor market will adjust to match supply and demand in general. For the good jobs, the market will adjust by raising educational requirements; for the bad jobs, the pay will be increased and the working conditions improved. Given such conditions, who can say that no more occupational education should be provided because skills are already abundant? Who will deny a person the opportunity to compete for the job he wants even though the odds are against meeting the goals?

Third, occupational education is tailored and provided for local and regional needs. Thus, while the national trends are informative, they must be validated in the local marketplace. At that level, vocational educators, community officials, and the employing sectors of the economy tend to avoid glutting the local supply with one type of skill to the exclusion of others.

Professor Thurow also contends that any labor skill shortages can be eliminated by information, on-the-job training, and labor mobility long before vocational education meets the demand. This may be true for the low-paying, unstable, dead-end jobs with frequent lay-offs and discharges. But it is less true for the better paying, steady, preferred jobs providing security and advancement. More impor-tantly, to assume that all labor skill shortages will be eliminated by informal on-the-job training is to belie the heterogeneity of occupa-tions themselves. Garth Mangum once observed that every job is ultimately learned on the job. But the only jobs for which there is customarily no formal classroom training either as a prerequisite to or an accompaniment of learning on the job are unskilled labor, semiskilled operative-type employment, and those lower-level white collar and service jobs that require only the intellectual skills which are consequences of basic literacy.

Both occupational education and the employer have a role to play in the training of a worker. The specific responsibilities of each and the character of the training given depends upon the complexity of the work at issue. But not all occupations are amenable to on-the-job training, nor should this form of preparation be even the principal mode of occupational skill development. Drucker would extend this point in his views of the evolving "knowledge occupations," which he sees as the foundation of the post-industrial American society. With particular reference to revitalizing vocational education, he contends that "the way to teach a skill today is to put it on a knowledge foundation and teach it through a systematic course of studies—that is, through a program. . . . We need an infinite number of people capable of using theory as the basis of skill for practical application in work. These have to be 'technologists' rather than 'skilled craftsmen.' "[4]

In essence Drucker contends that in many current and emerging occupations, the rapidity of change requires a knowledge base, not experience, as preparation for work. Thus knowledge, the syste-matic organization of information and concepts, is making even the traditional apprenticeship structure obsolete in many occupations. In sum, while Professor Thurow's emphasis on informal on-the-job training is undoubtedly correct in many occupations and in many settings, its cost in time and money and its complexity make it unde-sirable in other occupations and settings.

Professor Thurow also contends that every job obtained by voca-tional education graduates will simply be taken away from someone who now has a job or will prevent someone who is now unemployed from getting a job. This contention assumes levels of labor force geographic mobility, precision and dissemination of occupational information, and a matching of individual task skills and motivational structures which are theoretically possible but obviously unrealistic. While his remark that "occupational education is not going to be able to play the role that it undoubtedly would like to play in the economy" may be prophetic, it does not obliterate the social usefulness of occupational education.

A Problem of Substitution

Professor Thurow's second section, "A Problem of Substitution," addresses the concept of elasticity of substitution among skills and capital and labor. In particular, he observes that "if elasticities of substitution are high, one skill is easily substituted for another, capital can be easily substituted for labor, and workers quickly alter their laboring skills on the job." This is true in some occupations and at some responsibility levels, but not universally. It is certainly true that skill substitutions are high in entry level positions in construction occupations, for example, or in sales, or in lower level service occupations, or in agriculture. But beyond the entry level and in skilled, technical, and professional occupations, the incidences of substitution become fewer, the time to acquire the skills involved lengthens, and the need for a certain conceptual background increases.

Similarly, capital replacement for labor skills has its limits. Certainly, capital replacement, as when machines replace workers, applies in many occupations in which skill substitution is also likely. The substitution of capital or machines for labor skills is most liable to occur in the goods-producing sectors of the occupational structure. But it is less likely in many service-producing sectors where human needs for contact between buyer and seller or client and practitioner continue to outweigh machine efficiency. Since the service-producing sectors now represent some 60 percent of the jobs available and are still expanding, I am not sure how much capital replacement can ultimately occur.

Professor Thurow observes, "I am not a pessimist about the possibility of making accurate labor projections; but if the elasticities of substitution are high, it is simply impossible to make the most desired projections." I would extend this perspective. People do not always do what statistics or rationality would project. Choosing is often more psychological than logical. Having a certain set of skills is not assurance that one will use them in a directly related occupation or that everyone acquiring specific skills intends to use them as we might expect.

For example, we assume that 100 percent of the students enrolled in elementary education intend to seek positions in elementary schools. When we calculate the available positions in elementary schools, we realize that we cannot absorb all of these students. Immediately we talk of phasing out programs, setting quotas, and even eliminating Colleges of Education. But data collected at Penn State and elsewhere suggest that of the people enrolled in elementary education, only something like 60 percent of them actually seek positions in elementary education. One of the explanations for such data is that an education major receives a highly elastic, highly transferable set of skills applicable to many occupations beyond the public school classroom—for example, sales, administration, management, government, day care, child development, foundation work, industrial training, and personnel administration. A second explanation for the disparity between enrollment in a curriculum and pursuit of occupations related to that curriculum is that the choice of the curriculum may not have been vocationally motivated in the first place. Perhaps the student wanted a congenial place to grow in, to explore, and to acquire some reserve skills in case the marriage or the family business did not work out.

Next Professor Thurow suggests that "if accurate skill projections are impossible at the level of detail desired by vocational education, then something may be wrong with the degree of specificity of the skills taught in vocational education. The same factors that limit the detail that can be built into skill projections limit the amount of specificity that ought to be built into vocational education." His concern here has been debated within vocational education for much of its history. I would submit, however, that vocational-occupational education has been evolving strategies to respond to this issue since the mid-1960s. For example, since federal legislation has broadened dramatically the number of occupational areas appropriately considered the province of vocational-occupational education, it has become obvious that not all of these areas can be dealt with in terms of specific skills—and they should not be. Rather, cluster approaches to occupational education, training students in common sets of skills required for entry levels in particular job families and providing specific occupational skills only where local industries cannot or will not, have emerged. The cluster concept clearly acknowledges the elasticities of substitution at certain skill levels, but it does not abdicate responsibility for training people more specifically where local or regional conditions require or where elasticity of substitution is not a dominant factor. In addition, vocational-occupational education in secondary and post-secondary settings has entered into various arrangements whereby classroom study and on-the-job experiences in local business or industrial sites are effectively integrated. The rapid expansion of cooperative education is one example. Another is the development of employer- and experience-based career education models. It is wrong to say that occupational education intends to prepare fully polished, skilled workers for the labor force. Instead, most occupational education tries to provide people with sufficient information, concepts, and skills to make them immediately useful in many entry level positions and trainable in the specific skills required in more complex positions.

The Source of Labor Skills

These observations lead to Professor Thurow's third section, "The Source of Labor Skills." In general, Thurow's remarks here apply more to the recent past than to the stirrings of the present and the shape of vocational-occupational education's future. The "conventional model of vocational education based upon the neoclassic economic theory that the labor market exists to match labor demands with labor supplies" has been changing for the past fifteen years. This is not to say that vocational-occupational education is or can be oblivious to supply and demand considerations. But it does not follow that occupational education rests upon the assumption that workers must bring fully developed job skills into the labor market, as Professor Thurow contends. There are several alternative and interim stages of cooperation between classroom and laboratory instruction and on-the-job training that can and do benefit employers and occupational education structures.

Professor Thurow again pits OJT against formal occupational education. I am not persuaded by the content of his impressionistic argument. There is no question that on-the-job training is necessary throughout the occupational structure as much to socialize workers to the norms and expectations of a particular company or position as to train them in the specific job content. But the assertion that OJT can substitute for occupational education throughout the occupational structure is not supported by existing evidence. Further, the contention that one of the big advantages of OJT is that it allows the employer to create a pool of partially trained workers who can be easily upgraded when demand requires may be theoretically appealing. But the costs of OJT and the concomitant loss of productivity from both the OJT supervisor and supervisee require an organizational capacity unavailable in many work settings.

Large corporations may have the freedom of personnel utilization that OJT, as Professor Thurow describes it, can support. But small, labor intensive, marginally profitable organizations cannot invest their resources in comprehensive and lengthy OJT programs. They must recruit from the training pool people who can meet their needs with minimal personnel or training investments. Thus the issue is not whether Professor Thurow's observations are theoretically valid. They are. The question is their applicability in a heterogeneous occupation structure and diverse work settings.

His final observations in this section vis-à-vis internal labor markets, limited ports of entry, and the relationship of seniority to the use of learned skills are interesting and useful. I would not disagree with his arguments here.

The Comparative Advantages of Occupational Education

I find less to argue about in Professor Thurow's fourth section, "The Comparative Advantages of Occupational Education." But some of his suggestions need expansion. At the beginning of this section, he suggests that occupational education must recognize the existence of internal labor markets, the importance of informal on-the-job training, and the need to establish a complementary relationship with the latter processes where they exist. I agree with these observations but suggest that they may picture changes in occupational education that are already under way. With regard to his concerns about the need to sort out the "natural divisions of responsibility between formal occupational education and informal on-the-job training," I do not believe occupational education either can or intends to provide polished production job skills as its major reason for being.

In the remainder of this section, Thurow discusses the role and the need for formal education to provide effective work habits, discipline, general literacy skills, and motivation. I agree with most of his analysis, but would expand upon it.

Young employees often fail to find jobs, or fail in those they acquire, not because they lack or cannot learn technical skills, but because of deficiencies in other areas—a lack of information about work and training opportunities, a lack of knowledge of the real demands of work-employer expectations, poor work habits (absenteeism and tardiness), an inability to fill out forms and handle interviews, an inability to accept supervision, an inability to get along with fellow workers or to cope with the demands of work, and poor attitudes toward work. The maladjustment of secondary students in the transition to the workplace may, in fact, be more closely related to poor interpersonal skills than to inadequate technical skills. And basic literacy together with good work attitudes may be more important for employment than specific occupational skills.

Occupational education has a role in filling these deficits in its own right and in its relationship to other components of the educational structure. Certainly, the rapid rise of career education in America since 1971 evidences the need for all elements of education to contribute to the sorts of behaviors that underlie effective employability in a technological age. Self-identity, career awareness, economic literacy, decision-making prowess, and employability are all elements of a competent personality in American society. Such goals of education as these can no longer be treated as by-products of abstract verbal learning. They are worthy in their own right of systematic treatment. Many observers contend that academic skills and work must be treated as interrelated rather than separate. Darcy, for example, has indicated that the basic skills related to work success include communication skills, computational skills, manual dexterity skills, and skills in group organization and human relations.[5] It is his position that employability, productivity, and earning power are enhanced by verbal skills (reading, writing, and speaking), mathematics, manual skills, and the ability to work effectively with other people. These skills are basic, durable, versatile, transferable, open-ended, and elastic. They represent human capital virtually immune to obsolescence.

Marland has argued that interpersonal and organizational understanding are "survival skills" without which one simply cannot exist in a modern nation-state.[6] Coleman has argued that before a student becomes 18, the educational system should provide him with the following basic skills:

1. Intellectual skills, or the kinds of things that schooling at its best teaches.

2. Skills of some occupation that may be filled by a secondary school graduate, so that every 18-year-old is accredited in some occupation, whether he continues in school or not.

3. Decision-making skills, or those skills that help one make decisions in complex situations where consequences follow.

4. General physical and mechanical skills, or skills that allow the young person to deal with physical and mechanical problems he may confront outside work, in the home, or elsewhere.

5. Bureaucratic and organizational skills that allow one to cope with a bureaucratic organization, as an employer, a customer, a client, a manager, or an entrepreneur.

6. Skills in caring for children, old people, sick people, or other dependent people.

7. Emergency skills so that one can act in an emergency or an unfamiliar situation in sufficient time to deal with the emergency.

8. Verbal communication skills to be used in argumentation and debate.[7]

In testimony before the U.S. House of Representatives Education and Labor Subcommittee on Elementary, Secondary, and Vocational Education, I recently argued that a constellation of knowledge and skills important to educational achievement, to career development, and to work satisfaction and adjustment could be identified and need a systematic educational response. This constellation follows:

1. A knowledge of one's own strengths and weaknesses, preferences, and values, and the skill to relate these to the educational and occupational options available. The ability to make a realistic self-estimate.

2. An ability to use existing exploratory resources—educational opportunities, part-time work, books, audio-visual resources—realistically to test personal characteristics and choices.

3. A knowledge of educational, occupational, and social lifestyle options and the skill to determine the interactions among them.

4. An ability to choose—that is, to understand and apply the decision-making process purposefully and rationally.

5. Skills in interpersonal relationships—the ability to work cooperatively with others; to understand worker-supervisor relations; and to adapt to different people and conditions.

6. Employability and job-seeking skills—an understanding of applications and interviewing behavior.

7. An understanding of personal roles as an employee, a customer, a client, and an entrepreneur.

8. An understanding of the interdependence of the educational and occupational structures, the pathways between them, and the relationship of subject matter to its application in professional and technical vocational settings.

9. A knowledge of how to organize one's time and energy to get work done, to set priorities, and to plan.

10. An ability to see oneself as some *one,* as a person of worth and dignity, as a basis for seeing oneself as something.[8]

Not all of these skills should be the province of occupational education, but many of them can be. In other instances, occupational education will have to collaborate with general education to achieve these goals. Certainly, as Professor Thurow suggests, cognitive job skills of various types might be the organizing themes around which other types of learning can occur.

In the final analysis, I see a significant place in American society for occupational education. The great challenge for occupational education is to work out modified divisions of responsibility in relation to informal on-the-job training, internal labor markets, and existing ports of entry, on the one hand, and divisions of responsibility and collaborative relationships with general education, on the other.

Notes

1. Edwin L. Herr, "Manpower Policies, Vocational Guidance and Career Development," in Edwin L. Herr, ed. *Vocational Guidance and Human Development.* Boston: Houghton Mifflin, 1974, p. 34.
2. Advisory Council on Vocational Education, *Vocational Education: The Bridge Between Man and His Work.* Washington: The Council, 1968.
3. James O'Toole, *The Reserve Army of the Underemployed.* Monographs on Career Education. Washington: U.S. Department of Health, Education, and Welfare, 1974, p. 12.
4. Peter Drucker, *The Age of Discontinuity: Guidelines to a Changing Society.* New York: Harper and Row, 1969, p. 318.
5. R.L. Darcy, "Manpower in a Changing Curriculum," *American Vocational Journal,* March 1969, pp. 57–60.
6. S.P. Marland, "Career Education 300 Days Later," *American Vocational Journal,* February 1972, p. 2.
7. J.A. Coleman, "How Do the Young Become Adults?" *Review of Educational Research,* Fall 1972, pp. 431–40.
8. Edwin L. Herr, Statement on the Career Guidance and Counseling Act of 1975: Research and Theoretical Perspectives. *Hearings Before the Subcommittee on Elementary, Secondary, and Vocational Education of the Committee on Education and Labor, 94th Congress, U.S. House of Representatives, Volume 2.* Washington: U.S. Government Printing Office, 1975, pp. 962–1010.

Career Planning in High School

MORGAN V. LEWIS

If there is one word to describe the occupational choices of high school students, that word is "unstable." Studies like Project Talent[1] and the Ohio State Longitudinal Research[2] that compare the choices made in high school with those positions held a few years after high school find only about 25 percent of the sample naming the same occupation both times. Obviously, a percentage like this depends on how specifically the occupations are classified: as the classifications become less specific, the extent of agreement increases. But as the categories become less specific, they also begin to reflect aspiration levels or areas of interest much more than occupational classifications.

During high school, most students tend to assume career orientations rather than to make definite career choices. The Project Talent data suggest that these orientations can be arranged in a two-by-two classification scheme: one dimension being "college or non-college," the other dimension being "science-technology or non-technology." Employing even these broad categories, Project Talent found only a 60 percent stability ratio from grade 11 to one post-high school year.

Considerable instability also appears among students in occupational programs, who have presumably made at least an initial career commitment. Each year Pennsylvania conducts a six-month follow-up of its June graduates. When surveyed in 1973 (the last year for which I have data) 28 percent of the graduates held jobs either identical to or closely related to the occupations they studied in high school.[3] Moreover, I have some preliminary data, provided by 33 high schools in six states, that yield comparable figures. But these data also indicate that many of the students who obtain related employment at first leave those jobs within a year or two to take employment unrelated to their preparation.

There are many reasons why job-training relatedness appears to be so low. Certainly a shortage of suitable employment opportunities prevents many young people from applying the skills they learned. Moreover, many graduates who do not find related employment have not really made firm occupational choices in the first place. Instead, they select vocational programs as the least unacceptable of the alternatives available. They become bored and frustrated in academic courses, where they learn—if nothing else—that they are not the type of student that goes on to college. Told to finish high school, they find that vocational courses provide the least painful route.

If these students are then "oriented" toward occupations, why do they fail to prepare for occupations that appeal to them? The principal reason seems to be that developmentally most high school students are not ready to make career decisions.[4] When they select vocational courses that look interesting, they are really exploring, trying to find out more about themselves, and determining what they like to do and how well their interests and aptitudes match the requirements of various occupations. The typical high school vocational program, which requires students to choose occupational areas to study in grades 10 and 11, forces these students to make decisions they are not ready to make. The low proportion who obtain related employment following graduation underscores this widespread lack of commitment.

If occupational education were to pattern itself on the career development process, it would attempt at the high school level to maximize opportunities for occupational exploration and the inculcation of general skills. The problem with this recommendation is that nobody knows how to do it. Most researchers who examine occupational training conclude that students need generalized training that is applicable in many different types of jobs. They make passing references to "the communication skills," "an ability to receive and follow instructions," and "an ability to analyze problems." But most do not really know what general training is or how to conduct it. Thus they leave these problems for the vocational educators to solve. Unfortunately, there is no model of general occupational skills applicable to a wide variety of occupations for vocational educators to employ. In the absence of such a model, however, vocational educators do know what skills are required in various broad occupational groups, and these are the skills they teach.

It would seem at least feasible to use the seven broad occupational groups, which are the basis of most vocational programs, to provide opportunities for occupational exploration. Students could spend approximately half an academic year in each one of the broad areas, being exposed to fundamental skills and learning something of the day-to-day tasks that workers in these occupations typically do. At the same time, they would take part in correlated instructional activities designed to increase their competence in language, mathematics, science, and the other components of "general" education.[5]

But presented with these suggestions, vocational educators usually raise two objections. The first is that the suggestion addresses the industrial arts, not vocational education. Vocational educators see themselves as teaching salable skills rather than providing occupational exploration. The second objection is that as students grow older, their interest in exploratory education diminishes. The educators claim that by the eleventh grade, most students want to specialize.

My response to the first objection is that a program's label, "industrial arts" or "vocational education," is irrelevant. If students need opportunities for vocational exploration, then the curriculum should provide exploration and should not require premature choices. In any case, most of the evidence indicates that only about 25 percent of vocational students acquire salable skills, in the narrow sense. The vocational educators may teach skills, but a majority of their students never find markets for them.

The second objection, that the older students want to specialize, is more difficult to meet. The desire to specialize suggests more crystallization of vocational interest than the average high school student seems to achieve. To the extent that students actually express this desire, they probably reflect the general societal expectation that an adolescent *should* make a vocational choice. This expectation, though, is based on an erroneous conception of the process of vocational development.

These remarks are not meant to suggest that occupational education has no role to play in public education. I intend just the opposite. Public education must reach those students who are not academically oriented, and I believe occupational education has the best chance of doing so. In this view, however, occupational education becomes a *means* of making the total educational process more relevant rather than an *end*—that is, the teaching of specific skills. When Professor Thurow refers to teaching specific job skills as a way of getting students to "sit still," he suggests the same view.

If educators become more skeptical of matching high school training with labor market demand, the practice may be more appropriate at the post-high school level. Post-high school students should have matured vocationally; they should have more definite and realistic ideas about the kinds of occupations they want to prepare for and about their own capabilities. I know of no large-scale follow-up study of post-high school occupational training, but the Ohio State data suggest that plans do become more stable with increasing age. Nevertheless, the Ohio State respondents still express "a substantial residue of unreality in their occupational aspirations," even after four years of full-time labor market participation.[6]

Notes

1.   J.C. Flanagan and W.W. Cooley, *Project Talent: One Year Follow-up Studies*. Pittsburgh: University of Pittsburgh School of Education, 1966.
2.   A.I. Kohen, *Career Threshold, Volume 4* (Manpower Research Monograph No. 16). Washington: U.S. Government Printing Office, 1974.
3.   Bureau of Vocational, Technical, and Continuing Education, Department of Education, *Pennsylvania Vocational Graduates Follow-up Survey, Secondary Programs, Class of 1973, Volume I*. Harrisburg, Pa., July 1974.
4.   J.O. Crites, *Vocational Psychology*. New York: McGraw-Hill, 1969. For an extended discussion of vocational choice as the result of a developmental process, see pages 155–213.
5.   J.J. Kaufman and M.V. Lewis, *The Potential of Vocational Education*. University Park, Pa.: The Institute for Research on Human Resources, The Pennsylvania State University, May 1968. These ideas are developed in detail on pages 116–34. They are also reflected in the U.S. Office of Education's plans for career education. But there is still little evidence that these plans have had an impact at the local level.
6.   Kohen, *Career Threshold*, p. 125.

III
Education for Work: Certification and the American Class Structure

Certification, Articulation, and Caste

KENNETH S. TOLLETT

The current recession refracts the public's perception of the role of education in society. Pragmatic America has long viewed education as closely related to work, particularly beginning with the Land Grant Act of 1862. Yet it has been ambivalent and divided about the mission, purpose, and function of education in the United States.

Diversity and pluralism have dominated post-secondary education since the turn of the century. Thus in addressing the question of the relationship among education, training, and certification, on the one hand, with work and socioeconomic mobility, on the other, one cannot expect to find a simple, elegant answer. Thoughtful analysis of the question requires a review of diverse models of education, an elucidation of the purpose of certification, and an examination of the socioeconomic context in which education and certification operate. Such an analysis indicates that one needs a healthy tolerance of ambiguity and pluralism to answer the question.

Before discussing the models of education, the function of certification, and the socioeconomic context of both, I should state the question guiding the analysis more precisely. If credentialing and certification are, indeed, obstacles to various vocations and careers, a threshold question is whether these obstacles or barriers are rites of passage or substantive rational requirements to protect the public. From a legal standpoint, formal rituals appear to be irrational impediments to the acquisition or demonstration of certain competencies. On the surface at least, performance capability is the legitimate requirement. Thus rituals should establish that they are rationally related to competence.

While they appear to be more ceremonial and atavistic than practical, rites like symbols, and forms like procedures, may have meaning and reality more significant than objects and substances. A diploma or certificate, for example, may tell an employer more about a person's character, adaptability, and perseverance than about his skills and knowledge. And once minimal skills and knowledge are acquired, character, adaptability, and perseverance may *be* more important. Although conceptually and intellectually discrete, sometimes form (rituals) and substance (competencies) are operationally and practically inseperable.

In this discussion I first propose to review the present context of education, especially its social, political, and economic milieu. Second, I will present some diverse models, purposes, and functions of education. Third, I plan to examine the purpose of certification. In the course of addressing these three topics, I will give some attention to career education. I should stress at the outset, however, that a long-term view will be taken that undercuts the present reactivist, *ad hoc,* faddist response to recession. This view emphasizes the immediate practicality of educational curricula. I recognize career or vocational education as a legitimate, but not necessarily the most important, aim of education. A final note of caution: although I recognize that certification creates certain caste problems, overall I see it as the inevitable outcome of a movement toward a more highly technologized, industrialized, and complex society.

The Social, Political, and Economic Context

Education is emerging from a period of substantial social, political, and economic ferment—the campus disorders of the middle and late 1960s and the recession of the early 1970s. But by approaching the matter from the perspective of society, one sees things differently.

The social order in the United States as it moves into the last half of the 1970s is rebounding from a period of great change, shock, and depression—a psychosocial revolution. Most social institutions have endured severe pressure as a result of changing attitudes and lifestyles. One out of three marriages is dissolved; the desirability of raising children is challenged; and sexual mores have been revolutionized. Many women now see relationships with men as demeaning.

The role of the church as the repository of the value system has been shaken. The late 1950s and early 1960s saw the "death-of-God" movement. It also saw nuns, priests, and ministers participating in controversial civil rights, environmental, anti-war, and feminist demonstrations. Indeed, no social institution has gone untouched by the troubles and turbulence of the 1960s. Two forces in particular—feminism and the economic recession—continue to place tremendous stress on our social institutions, especially the family.

The feminist movement has brought a reappraisal of the roles of husbands and wives in marriage. Both men and women may be going through a mass identity crisis. The feminist movement also has a political component which will be touched on later. Identity and role specification problems fomented by social institutions in flux require special attention. Thus, in redefining their personhood and their roles in society, women are demanding not only equal pay and treatment but an equal opportunity to pursue post-secondary education or any other career they desire. Naturally this redefinition has had an unsettling effect upon the social order. One can sense a widespread urge in society to reestablish a state of equilibrium, whether or not feminism is, itself, a cause or modal expression of social disequilibrium.

Another factor influencing the social order in the family is the economic recession, which will also be discussed later. Economic recession brings both material and psychic depression. Economic stress disorients families and spreads insecurity. Much of the counterculture movement of the 1960s was a jaded, youthful response to affluence. Many young people were bored, then, with affluence and sought excitement and fulfillment by dropping out and adopting pompous poverty. Recession has changed all this. Students are no longer bored with affluence and secured by the knowledge that they can always return to it after their slumming. They are again preoccupied with attaining profitable careers.

The political context of post-secondary education is somewhat similar to the social context. The political order has reeled from the civil rights, peace, ecology, and feminist movements of the middle and late 1960s. The riots in Watts, Newark, Detroit, and other cities stimulated a longing for peace and normality. The four great movements, together with the riots, played a major role in determining the 1968 elections. By 1968, the anticipated backlash finally emerged when the nation moved toward the political right and its implicit conservative values. Ironically, liberals and progressives at the same time maintained and later expanded their power base in both houses of the Congress. The nation voted its mood or prejudices in the Presidential elections of 1968 and 1972, but it voted its practical interests in the congressional elections of the same period.

The populace not only identified the four sources of discontent with the Democrats and liberalism, but it also identified them with the social and political experimentations of Presidents Kennedy and Johnson. Educational reform at the elementary, secondary, and post-secondary levels was an integral part of the general reform movement of the 1960s. Thus the national swing to the right expressed not only a mood of retrenchment in the activities of government but also a desire for educational retrenchment. The desire for retrenchment in secondary education intensified with the busing issue. Education at all levels had disturbed the society and its political processes. Politicians were particularly disturbed by the demonstrations and other protests of students on various campuses. The public perceived students and their campuses as ungrateful recipients of esteem and funding. The academic revolution of the 1950s and early 1960s about which Jencks and Riesman have written so well brought a counter-revolution in the late 1960s and early 1970s.

The academic revolution projected the professor into a position of immense prestige, social power, and influence in American society. A growing economy and a burgeoning government needed experts and new programs and policies. Thus government and industry turned to university research and development to solve the problems that preoccupied them. The agitation on those campuses and the apparent failure of the programs resulted in a disenchantment with higher education in general and professors and students in particular. The dominant political urge was for society, as a whole, and education, as its vanguard, to become more practical. To use President Muller's phrasing, there was a movement to replace higher education with "higher skilling."[1]

For minority groups and the poor, the politics of benign neglect set in. Academics beat their breasts not only about corruption in society and government but also about the repressiveness on their campuses. A conservative President rode into office in part on the rhetoric of liberal and professorial failure. The government had been generous to higher education, but even the articulate spokesmen on the campuses themselves said that they had failed. Given the financial crunch and public disenchantment, why continue to be generous? Why not insist that education be more practically oriented?

The torchbearers of this neo-conservativism today campaign against government and power. Their politics parallels the policies of educators who want to replace higher education with higher skilling. The former run for office in Washington by campaigning against Washington; they pursue the most powerful offices in the world while denouncing "big government." The latter, unnerved by financial distress and by a loss of a sense of purpose, wish to transform learning into training, liberal arts colleges into trade schools, and higher education into higher skilling. A discussion of this loss of a sense of purpose will appear later. The present section concludes with a brief description of the financial crisis.

The United States currently suffers from the most severe decline in its economy since the Great Depression. Overall production has fallen, and the unemployment rate approached 9 percent during much of 1975. At one point nearly two million people actively seeking employment did not qualify for any insurance or unemployment compensation. Three out of four in the group not covered were either women or young people. The situation for Black workers was even more disturbing. By the end of 1974, the rate of unemployment for Blacks had reached 12.8 percent, while the rate for Whites had risen to 6.4 percent. The historic Black-White unemployment ratio remained at the 2-to-1 level indicating that "relative to their proportion of the labor force, two Black workers were being added to the unemployment rolls for every White."[2] Concurrently, inflation eats into the pockets of those who are fortunate enough to have employment.

This economic recession, coupled with inflation, has had a devastating effect upon institutions of higher learning. Southern Illinois University laid off a number of employees in the effort to economize. The City University of New York has discontinued the free tuition it established in 1847 and apparently its open admissions experiment as well. The New York Board of Higher Education cut $87 million from CUNY's $560 million operating budget, and Mayor Beame ordered additional cuts of $55 million. Institutions of higher learning are victims of inflation and of the governmental policies utilized to fight it. On the federal level, the current governmental policy calls for reduced spending, and this policy has resulted in a decrease in the rate of growth in federal support for higher education and in rising tuition.

The cost of attending many private colleges now exceeds $6,000 a year. Meanwhile, legislative approval of state budgets for public colleges and universities will mandate general tuition increases for graduate and out-of-state students. Contributing factors to increased college costs include fuel and energy, raw materials, and "inflation-ridden incomes." Since colleges and universities are labor-intensive (close to 80 percent of their operating costs are in salaries), the production efficiencies practiced in manufacturing are difficult to achieve. The large number of tenured faculty positions prevents the layoffs used by, say, automobile makers.

The recession in summer employment adds pressure to the educational process. Low- and middle-income students unable to gain scholarships may be forced to withdraw from or forgo college. The reduced number of students in some colleges correspondingly reduces the volume of funds received by those colleges. Hence additional increases in tuition rates. A 7 percent annual rate of inflation over a period of 10 years can cause overall costs to double. Thus a 10-year-old child of today may expect to pay $30,000 for a four-year state university education and $53,000 for a private college education. Thirty years ago higher education was a privilege for the few. Financial support for private institutions, where most students were enrolled, came from private funds. The lack of a post-secondary education did not block employment (at least for Whites). But the situation today is quite different. More than half of the young men and women graduating from secondary educational institutions benefit from some type of formal post-secondary education, and approximately half of the direct costs come from public revenues. The demand for credentials has focused increased attention on post-secondary education as the gatekeeper to economic and career opportunity. But the present economic recession may reduce access to higher education for those who are not affluent. Blacks and the poor will suffer greatly if higher education is left to fend for itself during the economic crisis.

Of more widespread and deeper seriousness is the tendency to equate the value of post-secondary education with its economic return. *Change* magazine recently published a series of articles depicting the lower financial return and the lower employment opportunity made available by higher education.[3] Right now labor markets in industrialized nations cannot soak up the ever-expanding supply of educated workers. Of course, the current recession has exacerbated this problem. A widespread response has been to articulate more explicitly and imperiously the relationship between education and work. This response has stimulated and reinforced the new fad, career education.

One cannot be too critical of career faddists if higher education has defined its purpose and function to be primarily to train workers for the marketplace. President Muller of Johns Hopkins has observed that "much of the public still believes in the college degree as a passport to the better job, and colleges and universities have done almost nothing to correct this impression."[4] College may provide these passports, but this fact does not define a college's mission or function. Education is partly, but not entirely, an economic investment. It should be interested in but not obsessed with career opportunity.

Diverse Models, Purposes, and Functions of Education

Economic recession and political and psychosocial ferment have pushed education toward a preoccupation with the practical and the financial while, at the same time, exposing the shallowness and lack of clarity about higher education's mission. Education can be viewed as reflecting various models, purposes, or functions. A model can be regarded as a kind of ideal description of reality, as a theoretical projection in detail of a possible system of human relationships—as in economics, politics, or psychology. The purpose of higher education can be defined as "the general design . . . for comprising the object it pursues."[5] A function can be defined as comprising specific acts or operations "performed in the course of fulfilling the purposes."[6]

One taxonomy of models consists of four paradigms: elite, manpower, open access, and universal attendance. The elite model functions like Martin Trow's autonomous university, defining internally its goals and objectives, as opposed to the popular university, which gets it direction from the public. Of course, the manpower model is entirely concerned with meeting the manpower needs of the economy. This model can be totally or partially planned, and it is the dominant model of the communist countries. The open access model is self-explanatory, although it does have such subspecies as "making it easy to get into but difficult to get out of college"; "having an open system but differentiation within the system" (community colleges, liberal arts colleges, comprehensive colleges, and universities); and "having an entirely open system."

Martin Bressler has set forth six major models of the college.[7] The six are scholastic, vocational, action-oriented, utopian, consumer, and experiential. "Scholastic" connotes a place of the mind, a time for thinking, and an opportunity for knowing. In Bressler's words, a student at a scholastic college is "preoccupied with timeless issues of truth, ethics, beauty, and the dilemmas that bedevil Western society: the reconciliation of freedom and order, liberty and security, abundance and security, quality and quantity, conformity and autonomy."[8] "The vocational model," Bressler writes, "assumes the redemptive power of work, and that collegiate education which emphasizes job preparation serves both personal and collective goals." Personally, marketable skills are credentials for obtaining access to possessions, power, and prestige. Societally, college acts as a staging area for assigning individuals to "elite positions and second-level leadership in government, corporations, and community." The action model indicates an education that furnishes cadres for the transformation of society. Thus knowledge is not a goal but a means. The utopian model exalts feeling, spontaneity, and improvisation at the expense of mere reflection, prudence, or calculation. The consumer model is similar to the utopian model except that it is almost wholly procedural rather than substantive—that is, a student is a consumer seeking gratification, not a future production worker. And finally, the experiential model is concerned with the totality of experiences which might benefit young adults.

Obviously, the manpower and vocational models tilt toward serving the economy through career education. But to emphasize these models is to ignore the others.

The Carnegie Commission saw five main purposes of higher education for today and for the future:

1. The provision of opportunities for the intellectual, aesthetic, ethical, and skill development of individual students and the provision of campus environments which can constructively assist students in their more general developmental growth.

2. The advancement of human capability in society at large.

3. The enlargement of educational justice for the post-secondary group.

4. The transmission and advancement of learning and wisdom.

5. The critical evaluation of society—through individual thought and persuasion—for the sake of society's self-renewal.[9]

Clark Kerr speaks of education as performing services to *production, consumption,* and *citizenship.* Thus education has production, consumption, and citizenship functions. Obviously, the production function, like the manpower and vocational models and the skill development purpose, is most closely related to the economy and career education.

Symptomatic of the underdeveloped stage of social science is its quick resort to economic concepts to explain and rationalize social phenomena and institutions. This takes place in higher education in part because of the self-consciousness of educators and the public about the extent to which the public subsidizes higher education. It is also a compliment to economics, which seems to have advanced further than most social sciences toward developing concepts for rigorous analysis of social processes. Thus one can discuss the impact of higher education upon society by talking about the "output" of higher education.

Output is a concept in economics used to analyze the production process. For example, labor, land, and material are all production process input; cars, airplanes, food, services, and housing accommodations are its output. Thus one can speak of higher education in terms of its providing or performing a series of services related to production. This production function of higher education involves activities which add to the output of goods and services in the society. In other words, "higher education is engaged in three major types of production activities which entail *discovering talent, instruction,* and *research.*"[10] To put it another way, higher educational institutions train people vocationally; they seek people with talent so that they can get educated and perform production functions for society; and they engage in research for the purpose of developing a technology and an economy that continuously expand. And of course the university can render consultative aid to the government and industry.

There is some evidence that the instruction students receive in higher education increases their productivity as workers in the economy. Although economic studies may be engaging in the fallacy of confusing *post hoc* with *propter hoc,* it may be inferred that some of the greater income of those who have attended colleges and universities indicates a productivity higher than among those who have not attended. (The *Change* articles referred to earlier do, however, raise some doubts about this.)

The talent hunt aspect of higher education has been woefully neglected. Higher education obviously plays a great role in providing students with an opportunity to discover whether they have the particular capabilities required for whatever vocation or occupation they have chosen. Related to this function of discovering talent is the problem of inadequate vocational and psychological counseling in high school and post-secondary institutions. Adequate counseling should help a student not only tentatively to determine his career choice but also (and more important) to select the post-secondary environment in which his capacities and aspirations will be nurtured best. Some post-modern youth in pursuit of a congenial campus focus too much attention on what Bressler called the consumer model—searching for self-expression, improvisation, sincerity, identity, and authentic community.

Although the research-service contribution to the *production function* of higher education may sometimes be exaggerated, the organized agricultural research of land-grant universities has certainly produced great returns in agricultural productivity and efficiency. The land-grant movement is one of the great successes in higher education and, for that matter, in social legislation generally. Unfortunately, no adequate research into the actual impact of organized university research on other aspects of the economy has appeared.

The *consumption function* of higher education can be seen in the activities of students and the campus community, which involve consumption of goods and services or the development of tastes, sensitivities, and opportunities that lead to long-range patterns of consumption among students. This function is closely related to the cultural impact of higher education upon students.

The *citizenship function* of education concerns those activities that relate to the performance of students, alumni, and faculty members in the area of civic responsibility. For example, this function completes a student's socialization. This function is, of course, criticized by many—and certainly by both radical students and academicians who feel that universities try to train students to accept society as it is. The public sector should be especially interested in citizenship. If educational institutions in our "democratic" society do not teach students about the American Dream, how can citizens develop an understanding and appreciation of it?

Professor Jill Conway suggests that the main social function of education—particularly universal education—has been the "preservation of social democracy" in America.[11] John Dewey, she observes, diagnosed the problem of public education as not having "functioned as an agent of democracy in America because it had taught the literary and aesthetic values of a European aristocracy." The public education curriculum was redesigned in response to this criticism, and the land-grant movement had already inaugurated vocational training and community service activities. This political or social function of higher education created the expectations and circumstances which have produced some of the disenchantment with higher education already alluded to.

I believe these high expectations are the results of higher education's former successes, particularly its performance in the land-grant area. Yet the universities seem to be failing miserably in their socialization function, if socialization is defined as adjustment to the existential social order. Current interest in career education suggests, however, a re-emphasis of socialization. Although my sympathies lie with the citizenship function, much of this discussion is obviously concerned with the relationship of education to work.[12]

Christopher Lasch and Eugene Genovese state that neo-capitalism must exclude large groups from production because they are economically superfluous—they must be kept in places of detention. Blacks, the new poor, young people, and women constitute the large groups among these excluded ones. This crypto-Marxist political, economical analysis of Lasch and Genovese is strewn with evocative insights and elitist humanism:

> The gradual achievement of universal education, like many other reforms that appear now only to have hastened the coming of the "technetronic society," was wrested from the ruling class in the face of determined opposition.[13]

Furthermore, the tendency of education since the seventeenth century has been to make schools into total educational environments, whereas the medieval concept of education saw a pupil as free of supervision outside school hours. *In loco parentis* developed with residential colleges that supervised all aspects of a student's life. Young people became segregated in a prolonged state of adolescence—a state of dependence and subordination. Young people in the twentieth century have been glorified in a manner similar to the glorification of womanhood in the nineteenth century in order cynically to keep the women, and later the young people, subordinate. "But," as Lasch and Genovese remark, "many women internalized [that subordination] just as many young people internalize the glorification of youth and remain permanently adolescents, emotionally, intellectually, and—not least—politically." Bourgeois society can solve problems of youth no better than other problems with which it is faced. Neo-capitalism cannot solve them without destroying the custodial function of the schools. Lasch and Genovese suggest a partial solution: shifting technical training to secondary schools and thus releasing the university from its custodial responsibilities. Of course that custodial responsibility is logically unrelated to the nature or place of schooling or training.

Lasch and Genovese further support the idea that there is correlation between education and industrial efficiency. Credentials have more to do with getting jobs than performing them. Yet somewhat inconsistently they argue that the most striking function is training an army of intellectual workers on which the corporate system might depend. "Higher education has become," they say, "another form of industrial apprenticeship." This makes higher education "another form of production." Thus the ruling class wants higher education, like secondary education, to train competent intellectual workers; to find compensation for powerlessness in a culture of consumption; and to mind its own business in matters of state. In short, Lasch and Genovese see higher education as producing intellectual proletarians.[14] This analysis appears to criticize higher education for performing too well the service of discovering talent and training workers for the economy. Also, when one assesses the non-pecuniary returns of higher education, one finds much evidence that higher education is failing miserably, at least at the most prestigious and distinguished universities, to compensate students for their powerlessness in a culture of consumption and to induce students to mind their own business in matters of state. Students were, after all, in the vanguard of the civil rights, peace, ecology, and feminist movements.

Certification, Education, and Work

Certain social, political, and economic forces have been pressing for a greater articulation between education and work. A psychosocial revolution has created role-identification problems resulting in more and more women pursuing financially remunerative careers through education. The same revolution has supported hedonism and a curious movement toward Bressler's consumer model or the "therapeutic campus." Reactive political forces and economic recession have propelled campuses toward a preoccupation with the practical education designed primarily for work. Thus colleges have become waystations providing credentials for travelers destined for money-making. Consequently the models, purposes, and functions of education most closely related to work or careers gain more influence over education's decision makers. Accompanying this development is a fear that certifying and credentialing create monopolies for the "ins" and exclude the "outs." To understand these developments fully, we must discuss certification, education, and work together.

To "certify" means to attest authoritatively or formally. Certification designates one as having met special requirements for pursuing a certain kind of study or work. And certification is often used synonymously with licensing. There are nearly 500 professional and non-professional occupations currently licensed by one or more states, and a number of others are regulated by the Federal Government. In addition, those professions and occupations requiring local permits number over 2,000. Inasmuch as the current trend is to regulate more skilled and semiskilled occupations, guidance, employment, and vocational counselors should alert students to the licensing, educational, and training requirements for various occupations.

Occupational groups began organizing themselves into associations nationally just before the Civil War. These national associations won legislation to protect their codes of ethics and their standards of competence and to maintain a roster of qualified practitioners. Furthermore, they gained the right to control or be represented on licensing boards established to regulate the professions of which they were members. Consequently, once a state association succeeded in sponsoring licensing legislation, other state organizations for the same professions followed suit. In addition, those who engaged in activities not traditionally regarded as professions began to be examined by the public if the protection of the public seemed to warrant professionalization. For example, tragic mine cave-ins and explosions created a need for properly trained mine inspectors. Thus the list of licenses for nonprofessional workers begun in the 1880s is still growing. Organizations have worked to secure legislation to confirm educational and experiential qualifications and to require a worker to pass a qualifying examination for a permit to enter a particular occupation. These permits can be either compulsory or voluntary.

According to Angel, compulsory licensing obtains where people holding the license are permitted to practice occupations and unlicensed people are prohibited from doing so.[15] If a license is required by a federal, state, or local agency, it is regarded as compulsory because the occupation indicated cannot be engaged in by those who are not licensed. In some instances, local permits are not really occupational licenses or certificates; they are permissions granted on payment of a fee that often provides a source of revenue rather than public protection. Exclusions from and exceptions to licensing requirements are always made for federal employees, and often for state and municipal workers as well. Some people engaged in research or educational pursuits are exempt from license requirements, as are students and auxiliary personnel working under the supervision of an individual who is licensed. Out-of-state licensed practitioners who render occasional services may also be exempt from licensure.

In some fields, persons holding a license can use a particular title or an official designation, while those who are unlicensed cannot, even though they may not be prohibited from working in the occupation. In other words, under voluntary licensing, the use of a particular title to designate an occupation, rather than the practice of the work itself, is prohibited. Voluntary licenses may be granted by national associations or by state and local organizations. Many employers prefer some kind of registration to none at all. An example of a voluntary law is the one that makes registration for practical nurses optional. In nearly half the states, a person may make herself available for employment as a practical nurse, provided she does not use the title "*licensed* practical nurse." Nursing associations throughout the country have sought to establish compulsory licensing for all related occupations. Nonetheless, physical therapists, psychologists, sanitarians, and social workers retain voluntary licensing.

In sum, licensing occupations and professions is partly a means of protecting the public. Licensing also lends status to those who are licensed and helps raise standards of performance as well as earnings. A legal analysis of certification and licensing indicates that the process must have some rational connection with a public purpose, namely, the determination of competency and performance capability. The question may immediately arise: to what extent do education and such credentials as degrees and certificates that attest to a certain amount of education rationally indicate competency and performance capability? Only in a few instances can it be demonstrated that there is a one-to-one correlation between educational credentials and performance capability. This fact leads many, like Sheila Huff, to suggest the desirability of expanding formal education requirements so that they more clearly and directly relate to work, careers, or professions.[16]

Before focusing directly upon career education, one should first point out that much education takes place outside the formal educational institutions. This fact was a major theme in the Carnegie Commission's Report *Toward a Learning Society: Alternative Channels to Life and Work.* That report indicates that much education takes place not only outside of the formal classroom but also at various times of the day and stages in people's lives. In fact, insofar as education is preparation for work, much of it takes place outside of traditional higher educational institutions. The report also suggests that, to the extent that these institutions provide credentialing and certification, they may irrationally and unfairly restrict job opportunity. My quarrel with this analysis and the emerging emphasis upon career education is that they overemphasize the work preparation role of education.

Education is preparation for *life,* only a part of which is primarily concerned with work. My position is based upon this particular definition of education:

> Education is essentially an intellectual process which transmits and creates knowledge or information, develops and structures critical cognitive powers, enriches and reinforces human sensitivity and sensibility, and combines the urge to explain, control, and reunite with nature into a purposeful pursuit of an understanding of the relationships between and among human beings and nature.[17]

With this definition in mind, I turn now to work, with some special emphasis upon career education.

One cannot gainsay the importance of preparing people for productive work in an advanced, urbanized, technological, industrialized society. This fact underlies the insistence upon treating education as preparation for work. Further, it has given rise to the career education movement. Recently much attention has been accorded career education. Grubb and Lazerson, for example, argue that career education is basically a reconstitution of vocational education. Vocational education did not work in the past and career education will not work in the future, in their view, for both attempt to deal with unemployment, underemployment, and worker discontent. But these problems are, they claim, indigenous to our economic system.[18] Although I agree with their description of what has promoted the career education movement, I do not agree with the implication that unemployment, underemployment, and worker discontent are necessary features of our economic system. But I do agree with the suggestion that these features be corrected through appropriate economic and educational policies. Career or vocational education is not the answer, certainly not in higher education. Not that higher education should ignore career and vocational opportunities in the outside world. Rather, higher education should be primarily concerned with the intellectual process, critical cognitive powers, and learning skills— and only secondarily concerned with vocational and career opportunities. Education should be sensitive and responsive to the needs of corporate capitalism, but it should not be dominated by them. Channels to life, work, and service outside higher education may be entirely work-oriented. But the models, purposes, and functions of higher education must transcend preparation merely for work.

Actually a modern, industrial, technological society is constantly changing so that training for a vocation or career today may be obsolete tomorrow. Grubb and Lazerson claim that students never really embraced vocational education in large numbers anyway. And when they did embrace it, they rarely found jobs commensurate with their specific training; and they were rarely better off in terms of income, employment, job mobility, and status than students educated in academic programs. In fact, they were often worse off.

Nevertheless, it is difficult to deny that credentialism and certification requirements tend to exclude from job or work opportunities those who do not have the credentials or certificates. Yet for the protection of the public, more and more jobs and vocations must be treated as if they were professions, sometimes to ensure minimum competence, at other times to optimize standards of conduct. A client or consumer may be victimized more by a lawyer's or repairman's lack of scruples than by their lack of competence or expertise. Indeed, it is the special expertise of a profession or vocation that aggravates the vulnerability of clients and consumers. Industrial and post-industrial societies compound this need for trust.

There is just so much fine tuning possible. As Mellinkoff has observed, "A distinction thus begins to emerge between what people who are lawyers actually do with their time and what they are licensed to do as members of the profession."[19] This is true of other professions or vocations as well. There are inescapable tradeoffs. Competency-based education and performance-related tests are responses to one aspect of the tradeoff problem. Yet one would not say that a prison inmate who devotes so much time to legal research that he becomes more knowledgeable about criminal law than many criminal lawyers should be permitted to engage in its practice. Of course society would not ordinarily permit him to take a bar examination in the first place. The credentialing and certification process, like the common law, should probably develop case by case. More and more careers and vocations will require general and specific education and training. Most, if not all, of the education may have to take place in traditional institutions. Much of the training may be left to alternative channels.

Conclusion

Social, political, and economic forces are calling into question the relationship between education and work. Much work is being "professionalized" in the sense that certificates and credentials are being required for more and more jobs. Whether these credentials and certificates are rationally and fairly related to the jobs' tasks is open to question. Work considerations seem to preoccupy everyone. Thus there is also a new movement toward career education. This movement is, however, of doubtful validity in higher education, which should recommit itself to general or liberal arts education. Credentialism and certification cause some caste problems, but these are inevitable in a highly industrialized, technological, complex society. Education is a relatively objective means of obtaining credentials and certificates, and in the long run, minority groups and society in general should be well served by practices that help people move into new careers and jobs by certificates and credentials obtained through education. The fallout problem of caste is intolerable only if access to higher and alternative education is not universal.

Notes

1. Steven Muller, "Higher Education or Higher Skilling," *Daedalus* 103 (Fall 1974): 148–58.
2. T.F. Bradshaw, P.O. Flaim, and C.L. Gilroy, "Employment and Unemployment in 1974," *Monthly Labor Review,* February 1975, p.12.
3. Richard Freeman and Herbert J. Holloman, "The Declining Value of College," *Change,* September 1975; James O'Toole, "The Reserve Army of the Underemployed. Part I: The World of Work," *Change,* May 1975, pp. 26–33, and "Part II: The Role of Education," *Change,* June 1975, pp. 26–33.
4. Muller, "Higher Education or Higher Skilling," p. 149.
5. Carnegie Commission on Higher Education, *The Purposes.* New York: McGraw-Hill, 1975, p. vii.
6. Ibid.
7. Martin Bressler, "The American College: Some Problems and Choices," *Annals,* July 1971, p. 57.
8. Ibid., p. 62.
9. Carnegie Commission, *The Purposes,* p. 1.
10. Theodore W. Schultz, "Resources for Higher Education: An Economist's View," *Journal of Political Economy* 76 (May–June 1968): 329.
11. Jill Conway, "Styles of Academic Culture," *Daedalus* 99 (Winter 1970): 43–55.
12. Kenneth S. Tollett, "Community and Higher Education," *Daedalus* 104 (Winter 1975): 278–96.
13. Christopher Lasch and Eugene Genovese, "The Education and the University We Need Now," *New York Review of Books,* 9 October 1969.
14. Ibid. This discussion is drawn largely from the Lasch and Genovese article.

15. Juvenal L. Angel, *Directory of Professional and Occupational Licensing in the United States.* New York: Simon and Schuster, 1970, pp. 17, 18.
16. Sheila Huff, "Education, Work and Competence," *Society,* February 1976, pp. 44–51.
17. Tollett, "Community and Higher Education," p. 278.
18. Norton W. Grubb and Marvin Lazerson, "Rally Round the Workplace: Continuities and Fallacies in Career Education," *Harvard Educational Review* 45 (November 1975): 451–74.
19. David Mellinkoff, *Lawyers and the System of Justice: Cases and Notes on the Profession of Law.* St. Paul: West, 1976.

Credentialism, Vocationalism, and Socioeconomic Status

SHEILA M. HUFF

In the early years of our country when few people received educational credentials, employers overlooked them as employment preconditions. Instead, job opportunities befell those who could demonstrate an ability to perform. Only when almost all the applicants had acquired the requisite abilities did credentials enter into employment selection.*

The approximate cutoff points for credentials are eighth grade, high school, and two, four, and six years of college. The completion rate at each of these levels rises to the point of saturation when large numbers of minority group people proceed through the educational system. But those who are already credentialed and enjoying a competitive advantage in the labor market begin to see their advantageous positions threatened. Their response is to make the access qualifications ever more stringent.

Moreover, employers presented with an abundance of qualified applicants can afford to discriminate on the basis of educational credentials. Thus disadvantaged people, always the "group of last entry" on each successive credential level, receive relatively few licensing and employment opportunities.

Recognizing this inherent discrimination, Title VII of the 1964 Civil Rights Act requires that educational background requirements demonstrate a valid relationship to job performance. When a particular job prerequisite has a discriminatory effect on a specific class of people, Title VII shifts the burden of proof to the em-

---

*This quick review of credentialism in the United States is based on various theoretical studies and unpublished papers of Dr. Thomas F. Green, Cultural Foundations of Education Department, Syracuse University. The author also acknowledges several helpful conversations with Dr. Green.

ployer to demonstrate the relationship between the requirement and job performance.

Litigation and voluntary compliance are proceeding slowly, and most of the cases involving educational credentials concern the high school diploma as a precondition of employment. (The requirement is frequently struck down, the Supreme Court's *Griggs* v. *Duke Power Company* decision being the most notable case.) Some of the cases have gone further to challenge the master's degree requirement for teachers. But the courts hesitate to remove this requirement despite its adverse impact on minorities because no suitable alternatives or performance-based tests for prospective teachers exist.*

In short, employers continue to rely on traditional measures of achievement—principally on scores of norm-referenced standardized aptitude and achievement tests and on the acquisition of educational credentials. And in the absence of alternative measures, the courts hesitate to strike down their use, despite clear indications of adverse effects on minority groups.

One finds in America today a tight connection between educational credentials and employment opportunities. Particularly at the job entry level, the lack of a credential can completely eliminate a person from the applicant pool. He never gets a chance to impress an employer with his performance on a test, in an interview, or in a probationary capacity. He is rejected by a personnel officer on his first appearance—or he knows better than to apply to begin with.

The occupational licensing situation is even more serious. Here, if a person lacks the prerequisites for merely taking the licensing or certification examinations, he is barred from full professional practice, his demonstrated competence notwithstanding. This situation creates a caste of exploited sub-professionals who endure low wages, long hours, and menial jobs in otherwise glamorous fields.

Consider the thousands of military-trained veterans unable to find alternatives to formal, accredited schooling and so faced with completing formal programs in order to acquire licensing and certification prerequisites. The enfranchised vested interests have, in many cases, gradually closed off schooling alternatives, thus keeping down the supply of newcomers and driving up wages.

---

*On this point, see Sheila M. Huff, "Credentialing by Tests or by Degrees: Title VII of the Civil Rights Act and *Griggs* v. *Duke Power Company*," *Harvard Educational Review* 44, no. 2 (May 1974).

Far from scrutinizing these social decisions, professionals functioning as gatekeepers simply inform the disenfranchised learners that their interests are best served by "upgrading," and this is sufficient for public acquiescence and legislative approval. No one carefully specifies the precise public benefits of such decisions; no one represents the interests of the disenfranchised; and no one calculates the cost and benefits to society of spiraling credentialism.

Dr. Tollett treats attacks on credentialism as a general attack on licensing and formal education—and just at the time when Black people are gaining access to higher education, securing better positions in the world of work, and beginning to benefit from licensure. But no one advocates the abandonment of occupational licensing. In certain professions and occupations, the public must have some assurance that a practitioner is at least minimally qualified to offer his service. What many observers suggest is that the criteria for licensure, certification, and employment decisions be directly related to the requirements for practice.

For example, the solution proposed most frequently is *more* education—not *better* or *more appropriate* education or better selection procedures. Just when various minority groups begin to receive high school diplomas, the town fathers begin to talk about requiring an associate degree for a police officer. None of them can show that the associate degree is related to being a competent, sensitive policeman.

To approach the possibility of "upgrading" through education sensibly and fairly, we need to develop a clearer understanding than we have now of the dimensions of competence in various occupations and a clearer understanding of how people acquire these competencies.

In considering the possible benefits and problems for minority groups of checking spiraling credentialism (beyond the threat it poses for those who already share in the benefits of licensure) one should distinguish between equal employment and equal educational opportunity. Title VII of the Civil Rights Act addresses equal employment opportunity, specifying, among other things, that credentials cannot be used as preconditions of employment if their requirements have an adverse impact on minority groups and their relationship to competent performance cannot be demonstrated. Simply because minorities are the last to acquire credentials at the cutoff levels, credential prerequisites for employment or licensing almost inevitably discriminate. Moreover, credentials are not necessarily valid indicators of an ability to perform on the job. Thus, if the Equal Employment Opportunity Commission and the courts could litigate all the cases before them and honor the letter and spirit of the Act, spiraling credentialism would be checked.

What would this mean for minority groups? For one thing, if they could pass the performance tests and licensing examinations, they would have access to good jobs. The lack of particular educational credentials would disqualify them neither from the applicant pool nor from licenses to practice in the fields of their choice and competence.

But on the negative side—and it is something that understandably makes Dr. Tollett anxious—is the fact that the emphasis on equal education might slacken. He believes that for all its problems in adequately preparing people for jobs, formal education is generally efficacious. Greater amounts of it eventually help a person—if not to enter the labor market initially, then at least to achieve career advancement generally. The more literate an individual becomes, and the more adept he is at mastering new skills and bodies of knowledge, the more likely he is to achieve an advantageous competitive position. Dr. Tollett's intuitions are correct here. It would be wrong to conclude that securing greater employment opportunities for minority groups by removing unreasonable credential requirements completes the work of maximizing equal employment opportunity. The removal of these barriers really does nothing to improve education.

(And what constitutes evidence of the successful securing of equal educational and employment opportunity anyway? If the good and bad jobs remain with us, one indication of equal opportunity would be the probability that the "least credentialed" and the "poorest paid" categories would be filled by people drawn proportionately from all classes and ethnic groups.)

The topic of vocational and career education requires us to look once again at what Title VII calls for. An employer complies if he selects for hire or promotion on the basis of validated performance tests. These tests must be based on careful job analyses. But there is little suggestion in the Title VII guidelines about how to conduct these job analyses. The state of the art among trained psychometricians is to conduct functional task analyses that require worker observations. Unfortunately, this limited methodology isolates the primary psychomotor dimensions of task performance. It does not weight the relative importance of particular skills to adequate performance. Moreover, this approach does not adequately evaluate the more difficult and probably more important cognitive dimensions of performance and does not show how psychomotor and cognitive skills interact.

Think, for example, about driving a car. Skilled performance here requires a delicate balance of cognitive and psychomotor abilities. An overdevelopment of certain skills may actually disrupt performance. Few researchers have developed a job analysis methodology that begins to evaluate this interaction and use it as a basis for developing performance measures.

This deficiency has important implications for career and vocational education. We measure with the tests we have available. A desire to increase objectivity and the overwhelming size of employment and educational pools have reinforced our dependence upon narrowly conceived standardized tests. It is hardly surprising, therefore, that the teaching of narrow psychomotor skills increasingly dominates vocational education. We seem to have developed a very deprived notion of what good education and good training are all about.

Employers are probably less naive than educators. Psychomotor skills may be a desirable addition to general skills. But when it comes to deciding between the two, employers offering semiskilled positions may opt for the general reading, writing, and mathematical skills. They cannot quickly equip workers with these foundation skills, whereas they can provide the psychomotor skills in a short time. Unfortunately, we do not have sufficient hard data on the actual preferences of employers regarding the general-specific trade-off to support stronger arguments for general skills.

Those who advocate improving the methodologies of job analysis and improving the resultant evaluations have the right idea. But even if the tests were fairer and keener, the lot of minority children would probably not improve that much. It might even worsen. If these children manage somehow to obtain credentials, they at least stand at the door. If, however, they fail to get as good an education as middle-class children, the keener, lawful, job-related tests will return them to the back of the line. The knot would be tighter; the evidence would be more telling; and the failure of the schools to contribute their fair share to equality of opportunity would be that much clearer.

If fact, we may now be witnessing, in its advent, a transformation in the rules of the game—a switch from opportunity based on credentials to opportunity based on examinations. Those who express anxiety and misgivings about what this can mean for minority youngsters probably should trust their intuitions. It is incumbent upon us to monitor these developments.

In doing so, we ought to pay careful attention to vocational education and career education. The only way to ascertain what "career education" means, and thereby to determine what part of it is open to liberal attack, is to scrutinize programs funded under the "career education" rubric. In the process, scholars and researchers should consult the participating young people and their parents to determine what they think they need. (I heard recently that adolescents in one of the government-funded career education projects got quite nervous when a monitor appeared on the scene. They apologized for messy files and for other inconsequential failures, and they remained ill at ease until the monitor assured them that he wanted only to observe and had no intention of reducing the funds. In fact, that nervous defensiveness indicated to him general satisfaction with the program among the students and the teachers.)

Career education was initially meant to be available on all levels of education for children from all backgrounds, and it would be premature to conclude, at least at this time, that career education is another kind of "tracking"—that is, of keeping the lower classes "lower." But we must be on guard against this possibility.

Vocational education, by contrast, was a creature of the secondary schools until the hegemony of proprietary schools and community colleges. Thus we should scrupulously determine who is slated for high school vocational education and ask whether he might be better off postponing narrow vocational training at that level and proceeding until he has had an opportunity to explore alternative career opportunities.

The issue is not vocational education or no vocational education. Rather it is when, where, and to whom it will be delivered and what it will entail. A student who needs specific job skills must learn them somewhere, sometime. Should he learn them in public schools, in private institutions, or on the job? Should their acquisition supersede the mastery of basic cognitive skills and liberal tenets necessary to move from unskilled and semiskilled levels to positions of greater challenge and responsibility? Is not something amiss when most vocational education tracks are occupied by children from the lower classes and minority groups? Is there not a problem when employers complain about the inability of incoming workers to read and write? What are the responsibilities of business and industry to provide specific skills? How should the schools (relatively uninfluenced, as they are, by production deadlines and the profit motive) be using their time? What have they to offer that cannot be acquired elsewhere? These are the central questions we must begin to address systematically.

There is a certain promise in the new job analysis methodologies. They have the potential for counteracting the quantitative orientation of those who focus on the psychomotor skills exclusively and promulgate tests and programs that define vocational education narrowly. Unfortunately, commonsense judgment on what it means to be prepared for life's work cannot, by itself, loosen the stranglehold of entrenched analytical techniques. Job analyses that take the interaction of cognitive and psychomotor skills into account are only a beginning. We must keep the future in mind: the prospects for skill obsolescence must be carefully calculated. The market for particular skills must be estimated. Most important, the twin phenomena of over-qualification and under-employment must be faced. The workplace must be made to accommodate intelligence, curiosity, and professional pride. We should also attend to such details as the skills that can be learned on the job—thus freeing education to train citizens in the development and maintenance of democratic institutions (including places of employment) and the improvement of the quality of life.

We are not currently equipped to meet the agenda. We are too disposed to rearticulate our general anxieties and vague misgivings. Too few of us have patience with detail, even though it is toward detailed, systematic inquiry that we need to turn our attention. We must take one chunk of the world of work at a time and submit it to careful examination, all the while guided by a philosophy of education that stresses equal opportunities and quality of life within and without the school and work settings. If this task were done well, our two worlds of education—education for work and education for the rest of life—could reunite. Moreover, our crippling educational schizophrenia, produced by early and narrow vocational tracking, would be cured.

Caste, Class, and Career Certification

PETER B. MEYER

One of the epistemological traps into which assessments of programs and policies often plunge is the acceptance of manifest goals and stated objectives as the appropriate bases for appraisal. What *are* the purposes of higher education in the country today? What are the *consequences* of those purposes? How can we move toward those goals in the context of a concern with new careers for which we educate in advance with uncertainty? These are the questions to which we should address ourselves if we are to assess thoroughly the alternatives before us.

As Russell Ackoff observes:

> Educators simply do not know what the students of today will need to know tomorrow. Therefore, they should not impose their conception of requirements on students. This is true even for students in professional schools.[1]

This observation is, in fact, *most* accurate for the professional schools. It thus appears that educating for emerging careers is probably all but impossible, unless training in the liberal arts enjoys a renaissance. (A liberal arts bachelor's degree is today, however, a mere steppingstone to the advanced post-baccalaureate professional training that high-level career certification requires.) Assuming, though, that educators *can* determine what specialized curricula will provide the best training for different careers, it does not logically follow that such training should be provided—at least not in the formal classroom setting.

The first issue to be clarified before we determine the potential value of further professionalization of the undergraduate experience is that of the purpose of education itself. The educational establishment has come under heavy criticism in recent years, as in this comment:

Today's school is modeled after a factory. The incoming student is treated like raw material coming onto a production line that converts him into a finished product. Each step in the process is planned and scheduled, including work breaks and meals. Few concessions are made to the animated state of the material thus processed; it is lined up alphabetically, marched in step, silenced unless spoken to, seated in rows, periodically inspected and examined, and so on. The educational process is considered to be successful if the final product can be sold at a high price. The system even puts brand names and model numbers on its products.[2]

The author of this attack, Russell Ackoff, is not a radical opponent of "the system," but an operations researcher and systems analyst at the Wharton School of Finance. He is attacking what he calls "machine age education" for its irrelevance to the "systems age." Much of his criticism of the schools is equally applicable to institutions that accept high school graduates and process them yet further. His emphasis on the systems objectives or motives reflects his impression that our institutions use marketability in their self-assessments and in their rationales for existing. Let us, then, examine the fancied and actual objectives of the educational establishment.

Reformers have tried to restructure elementary and secondary education for over a century. What is different now is the new entry of the education professional in the structuring process. But there is no reason to assume that the socioeconomic system will not continue to shape reform, even in higher education. The second section in this article reviews, therefore, the evolution of the "child-centered" reforms of secondary education as they emerged at the beginning of this century.

Finally, we have the questions of caste and class relationships, and the roles that education can play in reifying or undermining the divisions they cause. I draw upon an applied anthropologist's definitions to clarify the frames of reference I employ. To move from a focus on "primitive cultures" and race-as-caste to the more complex caste structures in the United States today, these definitions will need some elaboration. This elaboration will be the theme of the third section of this article, which relates educational differentiation and career certification to the development of rigid caste lines. For the purposes of future discussion, however, caste is, according to Downs,

a system whereby groups of people are considered to be separate because of some inherent feature of the universe which created the differences and from which there is no escape. In theory, all castes could be equal, but in practice this is never so. . . . Class, on the other hand, is a matter of different degrees of access to wealth and power.[3]

The issue central to any assessment of the role of educating for specific careers is the extent to which such differentiated education either alters access to wealth and power or generates perceptions that lead people to accept an unequal distribution of wealth and power as inevitable or appropriate.

The Purpose of Higher Education: Systemic Intentions and Inherent Contradictions

Liberal reformers writing about education often treat graduation as a stage on a path to social acceptance akin to primitive rites of passage. They argue that once all can pass the rites, all will be able to enjoy "the good life" equally. This pretty vision bears little relationship to reality because, as Marcus Ruskin says,

> the industrial system seems to be the exact opposite of ancient rites of initiation. In the ancient rites the individual attained the status of human being. There was a change in his existential condition because the basis of his culture, its guiding purpose and myths were revealed to him in a profoundly religious and basic way. As a result of what was revealed to him, [he] became a whole person. The situation is profoundly different in an industrial culture. Nothing is revealed to the individual and the possibility of his wholeness is explicitly denied through the Channeling Colony where the individual learns that he is to see himself functionally in the performance of a specialized series of tasks.[4]

A Danforth Foundation study of the economics of higher education, which, unlike the overly influential Carnegie Commission Report, predates most campus unrest, amplifies this observation:

> The direct role of higher education is most readily understood in the case of those professionals for which formal education is now the accepted source of training, such as medicine, engineering, law, teaching, etc. In some of these professions, the academic experience is a modern variant of apprenticeship.[5]

Apprenticeships *follow* rites of passage in primitive cultures. They do not *replace* them. We deny ourselves and our students the right to locate their "place in the cosmos" because we feel a need to categorize knowledge, and "when we isolate a subject, we inhibit exploration of its relationship to other subjects."[6] Moreover, not all apprenticeships yield comparable returns to their participants, especially in a society like ours in which no common rite of passage yields rights of participation for all members. Education thus is clearly a process that generates inequality, not equality.

A look at the record of change in higher education suggests that educators approve of this tendency. The Director of the Danforth Study observed from the vantage point of the mid-1960s that

> the general pattern of higher education and its internal division of labor emerged in the 1920's, matured in the 1940's, and reached old age in the 1950's. The two-year college, the four-year college, the graduate and professional schools [are] now articulated into a conscious overall state system, with specific functions consciously assigned and funds allocated by the state in accordance with this functional assignment.[7]

Characterizing the system of higher education as a pyramid, he goes on to observe that "the pyramid has become sharper with a greater proportional distance from the apex to the base." "The great equalizer" seems to have disappeared—if it ever existed. And why educators continue to accept their role as switchmen in the freight yard remains a mystery.

Let us return to the division of labor in higher education, one facet of the apprenticeship programs offered to high school graduates. Martin Carnoy notes that throughout the rise of public education in the United States, "The objective of schoolmen was to prepare people to take their proper places in the system."[8] Thus Jeanne Binstock, reviewing 52 institutions of post-high school training, found that "the college industry remains a ranked hierarchy of goals and practices, responding to social class pressures, with graded access to the technical equipment, organizational skills, emotional perspectives and class (work) values needed for each stratified level of the industrial system."[9] Moreover, the Carnegie Commission stressed the intensification of the division of labor in higher education, including measures to separate teaching from research doctorates. The Commission concluded:

> We recognize that some of these options reduce the chances of a common culture among college graduates within which people communicate. But this has been happening anyway, and we believe the gains will outweigh the losses.[10]

What could possibly outweigh a loss of common culture and non-hierarchical ties of social cohesion? Apparently the answer is production, and a social system based not on mutuality but on intensifying hierarchical control.

Reduced college enrollments today are attributed to demographic as well as economic causes. But I suspect that some 1850 observations summarizing the status of and attitudes toward higher education in the United States remain salient:

> Our colleges are not filled because we do not furnish the education desired by the people—we have produced an article for which the demand is diminishing. We sell it at less cost, and the deficiency is made up by charity. We give it away, and the demand still diminishes.[11]

To the extent that the manifest and expressed objectives of education are equalization, the educational establishment has been one of the least successful lobbies in the history of public enterprise: education has tended to increase inequality and to ration opportunity. This incompetence among the proponents of the educational establishment is hard to accept, given such powerful political and economic supporters as the major foundations. Thus to derive the true goals of educators in this country we must turn to the actual outcomes.

Equality and egalitarianism cannot be furthered by differentiation and division of labor in a socioeconomic system that allocates rewards unequally. Consequently the systematic differentiation of education, initiated with the advent of the mass high school and now progressing through the colleges to the graduate and professional schools, is wholly inconsistent with pursuit of equality through education. The differentiation in higher education is demanded and justified on the basis of the skill and attitude differences among incoming students. But this differentiation creates castes. At the same time, education's ultimate consumers, the employers, also demand differentiation. Unless the effort associated with pursuit of a higher education results in an improved labor market position for individual students, they will not attend an institution of higher education. So the institution, even if it does not discriminate on admissions, must (because of its market orientation) differentiate its products and thus discriminate at graduation time.

This dilemma can be solved easily enough in the short run, according to one observer of the education scene. We take the easy way out, says Ackoff, by "training our young in college to refuse responsibility for society as a whole and to retreat to their private concerns." Thus, as Weiss observes, the student is pushed toward a mindless apathy to all but his career by virtue of the structure of the college itself. After some feeble exposure to highly simplified snippets of "surveyed" professional knowledge in several disciplines, the student gets on to his real business of preparing for a trade or profession.[12]

The process is strengthened by the organization of "higher learning" around rigid departmental lines. The more rigid the departmental classification of information and training, the more isolated students become from each other and from an awareness of the real differences in their socioeconomic prospects following graduation. The more rigid the certification requirements for the complex network of different careers, the less likely students are to question their educational environments. In such a setting, then, the dilemma of avoiding input differentiation while providing output differentiation is resolved easily. Open admissions lets students in, and those who make the grade by virtue of their dogged study remain blissfully unaware of those falling by the wayside. Moreover, each student is so thoroughly indoctrinated to concentrate on his own academic problems that a tendency to ignore the conditions facing fellow students generates a lack of interest in the larger societal problems.

The price for the resolution of this short-run problem is the intensification of long-run tendencies toward instability. Because this short-run problem cannot be resolved without generating yet more severe problems in the future, the conflict condition is an "inherent contradiction." The inherent contradiction confronting education in a capitalist society functioning under the guise of a democracy is the need to *appear* to promote equality while successfully producing the differentiated and unequal labor power demanded by corporations and other employers. Students enter the educational system knowing that "one makes himself a marketable commodity by developing intellectual skills that have little to do with general knowledge."[13] They have been trained to demand specified, prepackaged learning, and they are thus projected into the status quo with a predisposition to ignore current problems. However desirable for the rulers of the status quo in the short run, this training pattern creates the crucial long-run problem of an inadequate supply of people with a sufficient breadth of vision to cope with the next crisis in the capitalist system.

This contradiction is irresolvable. Either the educational system starts to educate people (who may then challenge the inequitable status quo) or it fails to educate and agrees only to "train" people—

with the result that the conceptual skills required to adjust to the next challenge to capitalist hegemony will be scarce.

Historical Precedents and Perspectives

Efforts to forecast trends must begin with experienced events and patterns. One turns first to the past in the attempt to scan the future, recognizing, of course, that the behavior of people at any one time is a function of the conditions confronting them. The decisions facing people intent upon higher education today are not precisely analogous to the choices during the late nineteenth and early twentieth centuries. Similarly the job prospects and career patterns for graduates today are different. But it is fair to say that educators addressing higher education in the country in these last decades of the twentieth century face questions of diversity versus uniformity and of differentiation versus equality that parallel the issues reformers faced as high school attendance spread in the first quarter of the century. Gintis and Bowles, for example, have observed that

> around the turn of the present century, large numbers of working-class and particularly immigrant children began attending high schools. At the same time, a system of class stratification developed within secondary education. The older democratic ideology of the common school—that the same curriculum should be offered to all children—gave way to the "progressive" insistence that education should be tailored to "the needs of the child." In the interests of providing an education relevant to the later life of the students, vocational schools and tracks were developed for the children of working families. The academic curriculum was preserved for those who would later have the opportunity to make use of book learning, either in college or in white-collar employment. This and other educational reforms of the progressive education movement reflected an implicit assumption of the immutability of the class structure.[14]

While we do not now have immigrant children petitioning to enter our institutions of higher education, we do have internal, rural migrants. We still hear a great deal about counseling students to select an education that "best suits their needs." And we offer them a proliferation of post-high school and training institutions. The current analogue to the spread of high schools at the turn of this century is the "open admissions" pattern. But open enrollment tends to engender sub-B.A. degrees symbolizing a "new educational stratification."[15] Provision of access at the turn of the century was mixed with differentiation, and still is today. Community colleges are like academic preparatory programs from which high school students now transfer into college.

Another phenomenon in the early 1900s paralleling the development of "tracks" through high school was "an emphasis on school efficiency and the introduction of business oriented curricula. Efficiency [meant] the effectiveness with which the schools prepared students for work."[16] The American Association of Community and Junior Colleges appears to have intended to emphasize parallels with the vocational high school movement when it reported in 1973 that "career education as a concept can be the vehicle through which community and junior colleges undertake a fundamental reformation of their curricula to make them more responsive to emerging needs."[17] Whose "needs"? Obviously the needs of the students for jobs best met through a program of education that provides desired job skills. Providing narrow job skills in schools normally supposed to educate is nothing new:

> Equally interesting, especially after 1900, were changes in the actual content of the subjects themselves. The influence of commercialism and industrialism appeared throughout the curriculum. Commercial and business arithmetic, for example, began to receive extensive attention in the mathematics curriculum.[18]

Today we do nothing this crude. We just maintain colleges and graduate schools of business administration offering everything from certificates to the doctorate.

American educators have long adapted themselves to the problems of marketing their products, and have thus catered to the needs of the business community. In so doing, however, educators have sacrificed a great deal of their vision, whether or not this sacrifice was conscious. The emergence of course differentiation in the late nineteenth century corresponded with the entry of large numbers of lower-class children into what had previously been a partially restricted preserve—the high school. Secondary schools had been nominally open, but access was limited. The trend toward universal enrollment immediately produced a reaction in the form of the tracking system. A similar tendency toward universality in higher education was solidly in evidence by the 1960s. The system responded again: via tracking in community colleges. One educator, writing in the *Chronicle of Higher Education,* noted the great contribution of the community college system to the maintenance of "an egalitarian and equalizing educational system."[19]

The major difference between the turn of the century and now in the tracking and cooling out functions of education is the difference in the "room at the top." For all the expansion of higher education, we do not yet recognize a need for postgraduate education as an excuse for the lack of success of a mere college graduate. An analogous excuse served for a long time to explain the labor market conditions confronting the mere high school graduate. Another factor that has changed is the nature of the overall labor market and the tendency toward permanently high unemployment. As a result, the myth of education as the route to social mobility and wealth becomes more difficult to perpetuate as the percentage of adolescents going to post-high school institutions rises. This new problem may have precipitated an interest in furthering the process of "certification," a legal device for massive labor market subdivision. As André Gorz has observed,

> The line between academic degrees and social promotion could be maintained only as long as higher learning, though theoretically open to all "capable of it," was in practice restricted to a small minority. The traditional struggle of liberals (and in Europe, of socialists and communists) for the "democratization" of the educational system, turned out to be a fallacy when, in the 1960's, an ever growing proportion of adolescents won access to universities only to be eliminated in the course of their studies by new and arbitrary mechanisms of selection, or else to end up either actually or intellectually underemployed.[20]

Since such underemployment may stimulate dissent and dissatisfaction, a new rationale for inequality was in order—and the certification process provided a natural vehicle.

Class Subgroups and the Reemergence of Caste

There exist in the United States today both a class and a caste system. I do not refer to a caste system of Whites and Blacks, but rather to the evolution of the peculiarly American caste system in which "education, manners, affluence, attitudes about law and order and property, along with place of residence, become new symbols in place of color."[21] Samuel Bowles has written extensively on the role of differences in class culture as influences tending to dissolve any potential unity of a working class. I draw on his arguments and James Downs' characterizations of class and caste to demonstrate that new rigidities (quite apart from those imposed by racism) are generated by increasing career certification:

> Children of parents occupying a given position in the occupational hierarchy grow up in homes where child-rearing methods and perhaps even the physical surroundings tend to develop personality characteristics appropriate to adequate job performance in the occupational roles of the parents. The children of managers and professionals are taught self-reliance within a broad set of constraints; the children of production-line workers are taught obedience.[22]

All these children are working class—that is, they come from families whose members must work in order to obtain income other than from the public fisc. Yet they differ drastically in attitudes, values, and approaches to life and work. These differences may be required for the maintenance of a well-ordered work process, and may thus be intentionally fostered in the education process.

> The role orientation of the high school reflects the close supervision of low-level workers; the internalization of norms and freedom from continual supervision in elite colleges reflect the social relationships of upper-level, white collar work. Most state universities and community colleges, which fall in between, conform to the behavioral requisites of low-level technical, service, and supervisory personnel. [Thus we can see in the working class] the most complex caste system: separate occupation, barriers to intermarriage, restrictions on social interaction between castes, different lifestyles, and a ranking in which one caste is viewed as lower than the other.[23]

A great uncertainty surrounds the rank order of castes: the speed of technological and other changes makes it inevitable that the hierarchical ordering of caste ranks will change in the lifetime of any caste member. And so career choices and selections of occupational tracks in post-high school educational establishments tend to conform to caste lines. Admittedly, caste status is not immutable: an individual can move from caste to caste without the massive accumulations of capital required to escape the working class as a whole. Downs has noted that the major difference between class and caste, aside from the wealth distribution, "lies in the [financial] difficulty of faking in a class sytem."[24] But the increased estrangement of one group of educated workers from another tends to cause caste lock-ins: If the "common culture" (deemed superfluous by the Carnegie Commission) is permitted to disintegrate, then the capacity of any member of one caste to move into another will be effectively destroyed. Moreover, the more thoroughly we certify for occupations, the more certain we are to restrict inter-caste mobility.

It is time now to consider the role that this rigidification plays in

either promoting or undermining the social mobility which is supposed to be the objective of the educational system. The question is
this: Are people in the lower castes of the working class likely to
benefit from caste rigidification if this tendency is accomplished by
increased access to higher education and more career certification?
Part of the answer may be deduced from another question: If such
benefits accrued to the lower caste workers, what implications would
this have for the higher caste workers and for the relationship between the working class as a whole and the elite ruling class? Obviously, if the trend toward certification benefited the low caste people
only at the expense of the higher, then those benefits will never
come to pass. (People with power can be counted on to use it to
protect it.) We see here the major fallacy in the pursuit of educational equality through common years of schooling: as the percentage of people completing a given grade approaches 100, the value of
that attainment falls toward zero because the people who have already attained that level move on to attain more status and rank
through further schooling.

Many analysts now argue that high school completion (and increasingly a college degree) produces minimal net benefits because
the previously present "sheepskin effect," or the caste barrier raised
by that completion, ceases to serve as a differentiator. New forms of
differentiation thus emerge, given the system's need to have people
of unequal status—and more importantly, to have people with low
status willingly accept their lot. Access to the new differentiators will,
intentionally, be limited so that the lower castes who have just sur-
mounted the last set of barriers will always have "one more river to
cross."

No reforms in the procedures by which differentiation is maintained will ever benefit everyone as long as the differentiation helps
maintain unequal allocations of the benefits of labor. Except in instances of massive convolution, the reforms will never benefit the
lowest castes but will instead help perpetuate their exclusion and
oppression. Career certification is a case in point: the lower caste
people have access to post-high school training, and can even aspire
to becoming certified in particular occupational roles. But the choice
of curricula open to them and the careers for which they can be
certified are only minimally under their jurisdiction. Despite its
doubtful abilities to prepare people for specific professions, formal
education will now become a new discriminator. And those people
who could have previously gained access to an occupation through a

process of employment experience and on-the-job training will now be excluded because of the formal education-certification link.[25]

I have already asserted that the changes which occur in the apparent network of socioeconomic relations will be only those desired by the ruling class. This discussion of caste and class, however, has not addressed the interests of the elite in the internal relationships within the working class. Why do they appear to desire rigid caste delineations within the working class? A simple answer is embodied in the old adage "Divide and conquer." But there are reasons for fostering differences among workers beyond those based on race, sex, and seniority, which have sufficed until recently. "Internal labor markets" place a premium on the mobility of workers, and this mobility requires generally broad skills. Feinstein has observed that, outside of providing a common culture for a society,

> general academic preparation is also important for many jobs which require on-the-job training. This seems to be true in the business world, where employers often prefer liberal arts graduates to business majors because of their greater skill in interpersonal relations and quick adaptability to business conditions. [Moreover] general education makes it possible for people to learn new jobs when they are either forced out of the old ones or choose to leave them.[26]

To the extent that such education facilitates moving people with company loyalty into jobs as they are needed, the ruling elite should logically prefer general to career-specific education, even at levels beyond the twelfth grade.

A problem of control intervenes, however, in the process of maximizing the efficiency with which personnel may be educated and deployed. In *The New Industrial State,* Galbraith argues that the United States socioeconomic system has evolved into a creature of the large firms operating under the dictates of an advanced technology. He notes that the technology cannot be served by individual decision makers, but rather must be served by teams of workers, each specialized in some field, all of whom pool their knowledge to serve the machine—and the company. He calls the aggregation of these teams of educated, partially intellectual laborers the "technocracy." In his view, the nominal heads of any enterprise steadily lose power to the technocracy, insofar as it controls the flow of critical information.[27] If crucial powers are really vested in staff ranking as low as the mere technical workers, then the survival of the hegemony of the private capital system—and the survival of its owners—

depends on keeping those workers ignorant of the power they possess. Is it any wonder, then, that the "machine age" segmentation of education that Ackoff decries is promulgated and stressed? Is it any wonder that, in Ackoff's words, "children are taught to answer questions, not to ask them"?

Creative reorganization is all too easily stumbled upon in free and open team efforts and exchanges among people with different forms of specialized training, even in the absence of a generalist. Thus the teams that the technostructure requires could become very dangerous to the established order—they could promote "progress"—as they approximate the well-rounded and educated citizen Ackoff advocates. To avoid the creation of this competent intellectual body, the educational system invents increasingly complex caste articulation and career certification. Each member of the teams functioning in the technocracy, therefore, must acquire discrete professional certification. Each person must also be so indoctrinated in the defense of his caste that any intrusion of other team members on subjects within his expertise is perceived as antagonistic. This division of intellectual labor circumscribes any sensitivity to world problems by imposing narrow labels. It also ensures a level of dissent within the technostructure necessary to its control by the ruling class. Caste articulation and differences in styles are thus critical to the maintenance of the divisions of labor, which is in turn required not for production purposes but for the protection of the ruling class itself.

Notes

1. Russell L. Ackoff, *Redesigning the Future.* New York: Wiley, 1975, pp. 79–80.
2. Ibid., pp. 74–75.
3. James F. Downs, *Cultures in Crisis.* Beverly Hills: Glencoe, 1975, p. 82.
4. Marcus Ruskin, "The Channeling Colony," in Martin Carnoy, ed., *Schooling in a Corporate Society.* New York: McKay, 1975, pp. 30–31.
5. Otto Feinstein et al., *Higher Education in the United States.* Lexington, Mass.: Heath, 1971, p.33.
6. Ackoff, *Redesigning the Future,* pp. 91–92.
7. Feinstein, *Higher Education,* p. 21.
8. Martin Carnoy, *Education as Cultural Imperialism.* New York: McKay, 1974, p. 255.
9. Jeanne Binstock, "Survival in the American College Industry," unpub-

lished doctoral dissertation, Brandeis University, p. 6, cited in Samuel Bowles and Herbert Gintis, *Schooling in Corporate America.* New York: Basic Books, 1976, p. 134.

10. Cited in Bowles and Gintis, *Schooling,* p. 208.

11. Quoted in John Weiss, "The University as a Corporation," chapter 9 in Feinstein, *Higher Education,* p. 167.

12. Ibid., p. 170.

13. Ibid., p. 172.

14. Bowles and Gintis, *Schooling,* pp. 45–46.

15. Ibid., p. 248.

16. Carnoy, *Education,* p. 247.

17. American Association of Community and Junior Colleges, "1972 Assembly Report," in *Educational Opportunity for All.* Washington: AACJC, 1973, p. 146.

18. R. Freeman Butts and Lawrence Cremin, *A History of Education in American Culture.* New York: Holt, 1953, p. 441.

19. L. A. Van Dyne, "The Big City Community Colleges: Hope for the Academically Deficient," *Chronicle of Higher Education,* 6, no. 5 (30 May 1976): 3.

20. André Gorz, *Socialism and Revolution.* New York: Anchor, 1973, p. 19.

21. Downs, *Cultures in Crisis,* p. 79.

22. Samuel Bowles, "Unequal Education and the Reproduction of the Social Division of Labor," in Carnoy, *Schooling* p. 59.

23. Downs, *Cultures in Crisis,* p. 76.

24. Ibid., p. 80–81.

25. Ackoff, *Redesigning the Future,* p. 77: "Most professional school graduates cannot practice the profession they were taught in school until they have practiced it out of school in some type of internship. Most of what they subsequently use in their work, they learned during their internship, not in class." Obviously this condition applies even more readily to people entering the labor force with "professional" training at levels below those of graduate schools.

26. Feinstein, *Higher Education,* p. 33.

27. John Kenneth Galbraith, *The New Industrial State.* New York: Signet, 1967, p. 79.

Certification, Articulation, and Caste: A Societal Perspective

GARY P. JOHNSON

Certain predominant sociocultural trends have important implications for the qualitative nature of new and emerging careers and bear directly on the issues of certification, articulation, and caste. Among the most important appear to be modern man's interest in the acquisition and execution of power and the pervasive and continually expanded use and adoption of technique in our organizational lives. These two forces will be discussed briefly here along with their implications for emerging job roles and related work processes. Specifically, what is the fundamental nature of our present socioeconomic system and of its requirements relative to future occupational roles?

It may be argued that the primal motive force in our society today is the acquisition and execution of power. Power is defined here as "the production of intended effects."[1] This impulse to power exhibited by modern man is the fundamental determinant of giant corporations, unnecessarily large concentrations of capital, the relentless pursuit and implementation of increasingly sophisticated technologies, and the present degradation associated with many work processes. Further large organization, technique, huge concentrations of capital, and man's impulse to power may be considered interrelated and reinforcing with important implications for work processes and job requirements.

Regarding the predisposition to acquire and exercise power, certain intellectual and emotional distinctions can be made between man and animal. With only a few exceptions, the activities of animals are motivated by the basic needs of physical survival and reproduction, and they typically do not transcend what these needs make imperative. On the other hand, some human desires are essentially boundless and virtually incapable of satiation. As Bertrand Russell has noted in this regard, "of the infinite desires of man, the chief are the desires for power and glory."[2]

In developing this perspective, Russell argued that both Marxian and orthodox economists were incorrect in their assumption that economic self-interest was the basic sociocultural force, noting that once a moderate degree of comfort was secured both individuals and communities, alike, pursue power rather than wealth. He recognized and maintained that individuals and communities may seek wealth as a means to power, or forgo an increase in wealth in order to secure an increase in power, but he argued that in the former case as in the latter their fundamental motive was not purely economic in nature.[3]

Lewis Mumford reached a parallel conclusion regarding man's use of wealth as a means of power after an extensive historical analysis of the development of Western civilization, arguing that man now uses and views money capital as an abstract form of power and that power itself is the predominant sociocultural determinant.[4] This viewpoint and its supportive bases warrant further discussion.

In examining the transition to large-scale industry that took place around 1750, Mumford noted that a considerable part of the transformation could be read in purely technical terms (that is, the adoption and use of more and bigger machines), but he also observed a simultaneous shift in human motives through the increasing translation of both political and economic power into purely abstract quantitative terms—"mainly, terms of money." Thus, from an economic perspective, modern man has transformed a limited goods economy, once based on diverse natural functions and human needs, to a power economy, symbolized by and focused on money. As Mumford notes, while this transformation has taken thousands of years, "the process may be condensed in a brief formula: manual work into machine work: machine work into paper work: paper work into electronic simulation of work, divorced progressively from any organic functions or human purposes except those that further the power system."[5]

Such a transformation has been accompanied by the simultaneous conversion ultimately of human functions into *abstract,* uniform units of money or energy. Under these circumstances there are no limits to the amount of power that can be obtained, converted, and stored: "The peculiarity of money is that it knows no biological or ecological restrictions."[6]

Out of this transformation has emerged what Mumford describes as the Power Complex, a constellation of forces, interests, and motives committed to the relentless pursuit of monetary gains, in both direct and indirect forms and embodied in the large corporate structures that characterize modern socioeconomic life. One of the basic features of the Power Complex is its isolation from and indifference to the basic requirements of all organic activity, specifically human needs, norms, and goals. The Power Complex bears a close resemblance to a newly discovered center in the brain that has been labeled the pleasure center. In laboratory monkeys, the nervous tissue in this center can be stimulated by a micro-current, and the flow of electricity—hence the intensity of pleasure—can be regulated by the animal itself. Apparently the stimulation is so rewarding that the animals continue to press the current regulator indefinitely, regardless of all other impulses or physiological needs— even to the point of starvation. The intensity of this abstract stimulus produces something like a total neurotic insensibility to life needs. The Power Complex seems to operate on the same principle with the magical stimulus being money, according to Mumford. What increases the resemblance between this pecuniary motivation and the cerebral pleasure center is that neither admits of quantitative limits. The abstract replaces the concrete, and those who control it never know when they have had enough.

If we assume man's drive for power is insatiable, then one imperative looms larger than all others, the very conquest of nature itself. This imperative translates roughly into total control, which implies controlling time and space, which further requires speeding up every natural process, stimulating growth, increasing the rate of transportation, and reducing communication distances. To conquer nature is in effect to eliminate all natural barriers and human norms, and to substitute artificial fabricated equivalents for natural processes: to replace the immense variety of resources offered by nature with more uniform, constantly available products. As Mumford noted in connection with this point, there is only one efficient speed, faster; only one attractive destination, farther away; only one desirable size, bigger; only one rational quantitative goal, more.[7]

Several interrelated and mutually reinforcing factors have contributed to society's continuing advance in directions consistent with the conquer-nature imperative and its related postulates: the pervasive adoption and use of machines in production processes; the corporate form of economic organization; sheer organizational size per se; huge concentrations of monetary and non-monetary capital; and technology, or what Ellul and others call "technique."[8] Of these five elements, technique deserves special attention for at least three reasons: the use of technique throughout society has allowed man to experience, acquire, and execute ever increasing amounts of power; it has made possible the accumulation of vast amounts of capital; and it has profoundly affected almost every work and production process in our society, and thus relates directly to our more immediate concerns of caste, articulation, and certification.

Ellul defines technique as "the totality of methods rationally arrived at and having absolute efficiency (for a given stage of development) in every field of human activity."[9] This definition of technique is essentially similar in substance to H.D. Lasswell's definition, which states that technique is the ensemble of practices by which one uses available resources in order to achieve certain valued ends. We must now set out certain characteristics of technique that have implications for production and work processes:

1. Wherever technique is applied, a rational process is present which tends to bring mechanics to bear on all that is spontaneous or irrational. This rationality is best exemplified in systemization, division of labor, creation of standards, and production norms.

2. Technique is opposed to nature. Art, artifice, artificial: technique as art is the creation of an artificial system. It destroys, eliminates, or subordinates the natural world, and does not allow this world to restore itself or even to enter into a symbiotic relation with it.

3. Technique is automatic in the sense that it, and it alone, selects the means to be employed by its own laws. Thus technical activity automatically eliminates every nontechnical activity or transforms it into technical activity. Thus, from the point of view which most interests modern man, that of yield, every technical activity is superior to every nontechnical activity.

4. Technique is self-augmenting. It grows automatically, whether or not such growth is calculated, desired, or chosen. As such, it is largely irreversible. This is because technical progress tends to act, not according to an arithmetic, but according to a geometric progression, largely because techniques tend to combine.

5. Technique is monistic—it combines to form a whole where no specific element can be detached from the others.

6. Technique centers on the most efficient combination of elements, rendering every nontechnical (that is, human) consideration incidental.

7. Finally, technical progress requires concentration of capital, and this necessary concentration of capital has, to a large extent, resulted in our present corporate economy.[10]

These, then, are certain fundamental aspects of technique. They are by no means exhaustive.

We may now ask how man's impulse to power, the conquer-nature imperative, huge corporate concentrations of capital, and technique have combined and been translated into the organization of work and production processes. A partial answer to this question can be found by looking at the conceptual basis of present-day work organization.

First, there is the belief that for every elementary task there exists an ideal "best way," which can be determined in advance and independent of those who will be performing the task. Here is the first principle of separation between conception and performance that leads to the creation of special "work planning divisions." The attempt to find this "one best way" leads to the fragmented division and specialization of task; the standardization of tasks, equipment, and products; and the interchangeability of operators.

Job division and systematic skill minimization facilitate recruitment and place workers on the job quickly. They also cut training costs, minimize the personal role of the worker, and hence limit the risk of either mistakes or awkward initiative. Employee interchangeability makes the production process as independent as possible of, and immune to, unpredictable human variabilities. Thus we find a concentration of workers in standardized factories organized in rigid, hierarchical patterns.[11]

This conceptual basis of present-day work processes is entirely consistent with the characteristics of technique noted earlier, and surely not inconsistent with certain requirements of the Power Complex. That this conceptual basis accurately depicts operating modes in our present corporate society is clearly evidenced in Harry Braverman's analysis of work processes entitled *Labor and Monopoly Capital,* where he methodically and convincingly details the degradation of work and its processes in the twentieth century.

Virtually all of the crucial determinants in the degradation of modern work practices correspond to the conceptual basis of present-day work organization, to the technique embodied in our production processes, and more generally to large concentrations of capital. For instance, Braverman carefully documents how technique, through division of labor, has separated "hand and mind" in the work process, creating roles for workers requiring only the lowest cognitive and physical skills, and he points out that our present methods of production systematically destroy all-around skills where they exist, bringing into being skills and occupations that correspond only to technical needs.[12]

Based on the various ideas presented up to this point, certain comments can be made concerning policies related to educating individuals for new and emerging careers. First, given the extensive embodiment of technique in our present production processes, coupled with extensive corporate power and the high degree of specialization in our corporate production processes, the question of caste in the immediate future appears largely rhetorical. The new careers will emerge in coming years as a caste system. The question we must address is the qualitative nature of this caste system, which can possibly be modified or altered by the individuals within the system. Secondly, if the qualitative nature of this caste system is to be altered, our only hope in such an endeavor is certification and training outside the private sector. While this is not a sufficient condition to guarantee something other than mindless, unquestioning workers who accept the production process as given, I believe it is a necessary condition. And thirdly, career education, as it is now defined by industry and is being translated into certification programs, in both the public and private sectors, represents no more than a socialization process to sterile, mindless, inhuman experience; and, in fact, the process actually promotes and encourages acceptance of such a career context.

In conclusion, it would appear that the ultimate educational challenge we face today is the development of programs and experiences that somehow educate human beings capable of understanding their own nature sufficiently to control the forces and mechanisms that they themselves have brought into existence.

Notes

1. Bertrand Russell. *Power.* New York: Barnes & Noble, 1963, p. 25.
2. Ibid., p. 8.
3. Ibid., p. 9.
4. Lewis Mumford. *Myth of the Machine: The Pentagon of Power.* New York: Harcourt Brace Jovanovich, 1970.
5. Ibid., p. 165.
6. Ibid.
7. Ibid., p. 173.
8. Jacques Ellul. *The Technological Society.* New York: Knopf, 1964.
9. Ibid., p. xxv.

10.   Ibid., pp. 79–85, 184.
11.   This analysis is drawn from J. Carpenter, "Organizational Techniques and the Humanization of Work," *International Labor Review,* August 1974, pp. 94–95.
12.   Harry Braverman. *Labor and Monopoly Capital.* New York: Monthly Review Press, 1974, p. 82.

IV
Education Beyond
the Economic Model

Education Beyond the Economic Model

NATHAN GLAZER

The strategies of institutions, students, potential students, faculty, potential faculty, governments, foundations, and donors all seem interpretable in terms of a single question: Will those strategies provide an income-producing job, or won't they? So the question is whether anything remains in the broad term "education" beyond its specific value in giving people marketable and income-producing abilities.

We all know that education means "something else" too, but we can't find the conviction, the ideas, or the words to explain what that "something else" is. One would be wrong to think that this problem involves only those engaged directly in training people for work and careers. The fact is, one finds the same dilemma in the liberal arts colleges and the major universities, where classical and traditional ideas of education should be healthy and strong. The question there, too, is, What is education for if it is not for getting those engaged in it a higher income at pleasanter work?

Thus the age of reform of liberal education seems dead, just at the point where the explosive growth of career education leads those in these newer fields to ask, Should we be doing something more than merely preparing people for jobs in the most efficient and effective way possible; and if so, what; and according to what rationale?

Consider for the moment the fate of the decades-old effort to define a coherent college curriculum for undergraduates—or as we would now call it, the first stage of "post-secondary education." That first stage was marked by a number of phases. In the nineteenth century, college education, in both England and the United States, meant Greek, Latin, mathematics, and little more. The justification for this training, if anyone thought about it, was that these subjects encompassed wisdom. They gave entry then to the learned professions—the ministry, medicine, and the law. In a sense we could consider them early vocational requirements; for just as modern credentials require aspirants to some occupations or professions to study materials irrelevant to their practice but expected of the practitioners nevertheless, so too the classical languages and mathematics in nineteenth century higher education were undertaken for strictly vocational reasons.

Of course this analogy misrepresents the way nineteenth century educators saw Greek and Latin and mathematics: as the repositories of truth, wisdom, and understanding—both revealed and natural. Admittedly, this higher understanding may not have been shared by those who had to learn these subjects—one can envision a young man aspiring simply to a better, softer life devoting himself, without higher motives, to mastering the specific skills required.

Of course in the United States, the Greek-Latin-mathematics route to the higher vocations, the professions, was broken. Here we tolerated an unlearned as well as a learned ministry, as well as doctors and lawyers who never attended college and who, despite their reduced status, managed quite well. In time, the college and university managed to reestablish their monopoly over the routes to the higher professions. Medical schools, law schools, even theological schools were considered better, superior, insofar as they were parts of colleges and universities.

How did the universities and colleges manage to do this? They did it first by becoming more open to modern knowledge—primarily the sciences, but also modern languages and such new disciplines as psychology and sociology. Second, American colleges began to appoint (following the German model) scholars as well as teachers, thus raising their prestige. Third, the colleges freed the student from the two tyrannies of Greek, Latin, and mathematics—the tyranny of requiring substantial accomplishment in these fields for admission, and the tyranny of requiring the student to spend most of his time in college studying them. This curricular freedom went further at Harvard under President Eliot. Many thought it an invitation to chaos, and in a measure it was. The chaos could be checked only if one rigorously limited the subjects or disciplines admitted as part of the college curriculum and rigorously controlled who was allowed to teach them. If, as in the Harvard of President Eliot, there were only a dozen or so departments, then one could offer free choice without tempting the students to wander very far afield. In the Harvard of today—as in most large universities—there are perhaps 60 or 70 specializations, departments, areas, or fields in which undergraduates can take degrees. In many of these fields there are subdivisions as remote from each other as many of the larger disciplines are remote from one another. The dictatorship of Greek-Latin-mathematics had to be replaced by some ordering, and in the 1920s it was. The ordering was, in effect, the "distribution" requirement; whatever a student "majored" or "concentrated" in, he was required also to work in broad divisions of learning and the curriculum. And so we have requirements for work in the social sciences, humanities, and sciences and decreasing requirements for work in mathematics and foreign languages.

The American college curriculum was fixed 50 years ago. It reflected the end of the dominance of the Renaissance model of appropriate secular education and the enormous expansion of learning and science. And it proposed a compromise: something would be required (for the notion of an educated man would not be abandoned) but not much aside from "distribution."[1]

We have since had what can only be called a series of little rebellions against this model. In some cases the rebellions required a fixed curriculum, like St. John's "Great Books," Meiklejohn's Experimental College at the University of Wisconsin, and the latter's revival by Joseph Tussman at Berkeley.[2] We have also had one more substantial line of development in the attempt to create a curriculum suited for contemporary times: Contemporary Civilization at Columbia, the College of the University of Chicago, and the abortive General Education Program at Harvard—all chronicled by Daniel Bell.[3] They have all emerged as slightly different versions of the distribution requirement. Finally, rebellions have attacked even the last remnants of the attempt to establish in a modern curriculum a definition of the educated man—a contemporary equivalent of Greek-Latin-mathematics. These rebellions reflect a long-range secular trend toward the demise of any notion of the curriculum.

And it is hard to see how that trend—in general education, in liberal education, in "education beyond the economic model"—can be reversed. The University of California at Berkeley established a select committee on education after the upsurge of student disorders in 1964 and 1965.[4] Its report is another ripple in the general tide toward greater freedom in the curriculum. The Dean of the Faculty of Arts and Sciences at Harvard, Henry Rosovsky, established a group of task forces in 1976. One of them deals with general education, considered a major Harvard innovation in trouble for many years. Another deals with "concentrations," as Harvard calls its majors. There is no hint what these committees will decide, but new ideas no longer spring full blown from the brow of Jove, so one suspects that the reports will do little to stem the decay of general education and the liberal curriculum. One can further guess, since Harvard in 1976 is different from Berkeley in 1966, that they will offer an argument for holding the line roughly at the present front where a good deal of distribution is still required of the undergraduates. There may even be some small movement toward more extensive or stronger requirements.

I review this history of efforts to establish a general education or liberal education for undergraduate students because it would seem to be a first step in asking what form of education, beyond that most directly suitable for careers, we should require in the burgeoning new programs of career education. What can we justify beyond that which directly qualifies or certifies a person to fill a given role or perform a suitable task? If we have difficulty establishing a general education requirement for the student in a liberal four-year college, we would have even greater difficulty establishing a similar requirement for students in career-oriented education. And indeed, so we do.

Why, then, should this kind of education be offered in a college at all? It is not an easy question. Abraham Flexner was able to argue that medicine should be taught in universities and drove practically every medical school not connected with a university out of business. Nevertheless, medical schools remain separate from whatever else goes on in a university. Indeed, in two universities I have been connected with, the University of California at Berkeley and Harvard, the medical schools are located across bodies of water (broader in the West, narrower in the East); they run on their own timetables; and they pose many problems for the organization of the universities. (For example, you must pay medical professors more, and you have to appoint numerous "adjunct" faculty members whose relationship to the university is liable to be irregular.) Similarly, while the most prestigious law schools are associated with universities, in both universities where I have taught the law faculties insist on setting their own calendars, which makes it hard either for regular students to take their courses or for their students to take outside courses. When we examine the less exalted professions—for example, nursing or optometry—we find weaker arguments for university affiliation. Non-university education in the professions is usually cheaper, and I have heard of no evidence to show it is worse. Certainly non-university education in the newer professions presumably is both cheaper and shorter. It is unhampered by institutional rules, requirements, and limitations irrelevant to the simple career training function, and as the domain of independent institutions, it can address itself to whatever is needed.

Indeed, there is much to be said for the "disaggregation" of the functions of higher education, a notion urged by George Weathersby. At present, colleges evaluate past performance, advise students, instruct them in specific skills, test them for achievement, and distribute credentials. Why not separate institutions to evaluate, advise, counsel, instruct, test, and certify? Might not each specialized institution do a better job? And might not the problem of education "beyond the economic model" disappear? Even if one of the specific skills desired were to reside in some traditional field of the liberal arts independent of any economic function, it could, like any other kind of instruction, be contracted for. One can even imagine, in this world of disaggregated education, an institution that would provide educational "consumption benefits" (the kind economists ignore in considering the returns on a college education). It would be a college without anything else: dormitories where people could eat and sleep and hold bull sessions and drink sherry or beer and cheer football teams and have homecoming events, all unencumbered by professors and classes. These consumption benefits might even be provided on a grander scale than they are in the present colleges.

We already employ this disaggregated approach to providing the benefits of education in our present-day career planning both outside the university and in it. What is wrong, if anything? What more is needed? The arguments for education beyond the economic model cannot easily escape from the economic model itself. We hear the argument that occupations change; that training for occupations may be too limiting to serve for a lifetime, or even for part of a lifetime; and that people must become more broadly gauged, with a greater range of talents than training for a single occupation provides. And general education may provide that necessary range and flexibility. It may not provide Chaucer and Shakespeare, but perhaps it will teach people to read and write and speak effectively; perhaps not political philosophy, but the structure of government; perhaps not social theory, but changing social trends (which tell you where the markets are). And it will help procure grants. The supporters of liberal education themselves find it hard to go beyond such arguments.

Two more arguments one hears for liberal education supplemented by training also have economic dimensions, though perhaps not as direct as this first. One often hears that since man lives not by work alone, but through recreation and the enjoyment of culture as well, education should add these dimensions to his life. In its pure form, this is clearly an argument for "education beyond the economic model." But as we all know, an economic dimension argument often intrudes on this argument: one's work will be enhanced if one is skilled in the consumption of higher culture because this skill facilitates social interchange (and economic transactions), and it frees one for more effective economic activity.

Finally, one hears another argument for "education beyond the economic model": What will we do with all those people educated to teach English, humanities, foreign languages and literature, and the social sciences, and with all those institutions that employ these people, if we limit education to the training necessary to perform a narrowly defined task? Here the problem is the economy of higher education in general. It is a major industry; it is threatened; one way of dealing with the threat is to move into career education. But can it, in so doing, jettison all the commitments of the past—commitments that include general and liberal education?

Clearly the strongest supporters of general and liberal education must spurn these instrumental arguments. They must argue broadly that general and liberal educations enable man to fulfill himself, that they involve the transmission of the highest and best achievements and aspirations of man, and that it is impossible to discard them simply because they do not build income. Or rather, whether or not liberal and general education build income, the supporters would argue, is irrelevant: they are simply essential.

The problem with this argument is that the supporters of general education are not sure just *what* in the long history of human achievement in the arts and sciences should or must be transmitted. Nor can they argue that this transmission is essential to becoming a good man or citizen. Moreover, they are challenged by radically new and different views of what general and liberal educations require.

As to the first problem, that those of us in education no longer agree about what is essential: we can no longer resort to tradition. Because Greek and Latin literature was the essential education of those few of our forefathers who received a liberal education, must we limit ourselves to that? To some extent a new canon, of works from the Middle Ages, the Renaissance, the Reformation, and the great seventeenth, eighteenth, and nineteenth centuries, has been created. Yet we are troubled by the problem of the rise of new areas of the world making claims for their literature and art and religion, and even of the claims of science to become part of our general education curriculum. Undoubtedly there is a major tradition of Chinese, Indian, Japanese, and Islamic literature. Africa makes its claims too: 11 percent of our citizens are of African descent, but it is hard to know what to add to our overburdened general education from that continent. Latin America makes its claims, not only because it is part of the world but also because many of our citizens come from that part. Modernity makes its claims. And how modern should one be? Up to Yeats? to Robert Lowell? or to Allen Ginsberg? The questions seem unanswerable.

In an interesting series of articles in *Fortune* on "Education for a World of Work," Walter Guzzardi, Jr., asks, "Will anybody read Chaucer in 1990?"[5] That is the question. Some people ask it sadly; some briskly insist it doesn't matter. But no one seems to be able to make a strong case for Chaucer.

We can argue that liberal education makes a better person. But we can't prove it. After all, the United States, most of us believe, was a moral society (or at any rate had greater morale) when fewer people went to college. If going to college helps people get better, it is not easy to prove it—certainly not in a time when we have begun to doubt that it pays to spend more on education in general or that it pays to have more of a better education in general.

The final challenge to liberal education is the argument that whatever liberal education did to make people better—to get them to understand the springs of human conduct, the limits and possibilities of greatness, the nature of social groups and social interaction—can be done better today through direct teaching, training, and experience. Rather than read Shakespeare, let us organize T-groups, or attend night court, or visit a state hospital. Rather than read ancient history, let students discover or recreate family histories. Instead of reading de Tocqueville, Marx, Durkheim, and Weber, let them make a social survey of their block. It is not easy to argue with these contemporary approaches to general education if one is interested in achieving the statable objectives which general education is expected to fulfill.

Nor should one forget that career training also occurs *after* college education, even though it may assume or require a college degree. That kind of career training can be directed to specific and concrete objectives. While it is true that even professional schools may employ a few humanists or social scientists, one assumes that whatever can be done in general education has already been done in college. The higher professional school or the specialized career institute that admits college graduates need not worry about "education beyond the economic model."

The second problem involves career training in either the community college or the four-year college. Here the problem is more acute. One might, of course, assume that whatever part of general education is necessary has already been acquired in high school. European colleges and universities make this assumption, and it is a fair assumption in countries where secondary schools have a tradition of strong and rigorous education. We cannot, however, make that assumption in this country. As more and more college educations are broken into a year here and a year there, or a course here and a course there, a coming and going over many years, the question of the responsibility for general education becomes an increasingly difficult one to solve.

Finally, we can even raise the question of the role of general education in the high school years. As we reduced the dropout rate to 20 percent of the high school cohort, we came to realize that many of those being graduated from high school are unable to read or calculate. We realize, too, that general education seems to have failed not only the dropout but also many of the graduates. One approach to making high school education more palatable and useful is to link it with work opportunities, but this approach further reduces the role of general education. Perhaps the decline of general education in high school (whether because of faulty preparation or a desire to make the curriculum more palatable) is the most serious matter of all.

In the discussions that follow this one, Albert Lorente suggests that American labor has never limited itself to a concern for career education alone: it has always advocated general education and sees general education as good for making citizens, for making happy and fulfilled people, and even for making more competent and effective workers. Mr. Lorente supports the requirement for competence in reading, writing, and calculation; this much education *must* do. My particular concern is for the great tradition of higher education, for culture, and for studies that cannot be clearly related to economic effectiveness, to leisure pursuits, or even to good citizenship. I doubt it can be shown that those with a broader, classically liberal education are better citizens for that reason alone.

Dr. Wise worries that the schools are under attack for not doing a good job of education in basic skills and in broader educational areas. She says they are doing better than before. But I would tend to agree with Mr. Lorente that the urgent issue is not the defense of the schools as they are but coming to grips with their inadequacies, which seem to be numerous.

With Professor Johnson, I favor "education beyond the economic model." I am for it; I delight in it; I believe all people should have it. But having said that, I consider the prospects rather bleak that those who think as we do can bring forward enough forceful arguments to restore or recreate a broadly accepted general education based on the classic achievements of the human spirit. When higher education was more thoroughly rooted in the classics, (1) the students involved usually had vocational objectives, and (2) this classical education itself eventually came under strong attack from, among others, John Dewey. Professor Johnson does not defend this classical education, but he says that those who offered it knew there was a problem and tried to find an answer. I agree with him here, but I disagree that a new and more effective answer can be found today. President Eliot and other reformers were responding to strong realities that have become stronger: the rise of science; the critical examination of classic sources; and the growth of a more complex economy with many more occupational roles, each based on different specializations. And new elements have been added: the challenge to the primacy of purely Western materials in a classical education; the significant argument (stemming from Dewey) that direct experience should become a basic part of the curriculum; the expansion of higher education to encompass half or more of the population reaching college age; and the serious question of what general education may be suitable for and accessible to such a large part of the population. Undoubtedly it wants something rather different from what served a small percentage of the population.

What, then, can one say of "education beyond the economic model"? In the face of all these difficulties, after considering the fate of various general education reforms, and knowing the pressures to add even more direct work-education in the colleges and high schools, one can reiterate a call for more general education, more moral education, and a stronger common base of understanding, knowledge, and ethics for all. But no one is answering these calls. Society is already too splintered, particularly in its values, to construct for itself a common educational base.

I have just seen the motion picture *Taxi Driver,* surely one of the better statements on contemporary American society. What values are expressed in this movie and the dozens like it? Only the most chaotic values. Some of us know what we want to teach such a society. Certainly Professor Johnson seems to feel *he* knows. But if he developed his ideas further, I think from the hints he drops that he and I, both supporters of a basic general education, would have a real disagreement. That disagreement, however, is in the future. For now, how can we get people to listen? And having listened, will they agree to any concrete program?

And so I resort to two elements we all agree on: we are citizens of a good society and should know enough to be better citizens; and in a pluralistic society every variant of education should be encouraged—among them, the kind of education that links us to the great achievements of the human mind and spirit. I suspect that in a divided and pluralized society in which practically all the former verities are challenged, in which religion is confused, and in which traditional morality and values find few effective spokesmen, there are two courses to follow.

First, there is an unquestioned residue of education necessary for citizenship in some of those "traditional" subjects. As a democratic society, we must understand—to an exceptional degree even among other democracies—old matters. We have to understand the Constitution, and the origins and development of the Republic, not out of piety but because in our way of government they are essential matters. New citizens are expected to know something about American history, the Constitution, and American government. States demand that education in these subjects be given in elementary schools, in high schools, and sometimes even in state colleges and universities. There is thus a consensus that this much is necessary. And it is hardly challengeable when the interpretation of such phrases as "due process," "equal protection under the law," and "the establishment of religion" shapes our daily lives.

Strangely enough, this simple *instrumental* requirement that a citizen know something of his country, how it came to be, and how it was shaped and is governed places one squarely into eighteenth-century language, thought, history, and philosophy. Indeed, it pushes one into earlier centuries than that. I begin with this minimal justification for liberal education because it is clear and relatively precise. No one can argue that it is not essential for every man and woman; we have, in fact, written this requirement into our laws.

There is a second course which can go far beyond this absolute minimal requirement. That is to accept the fact that the consensus over general education is irreparably broken, yet to support whatever variants of it which various institutions find desirable to maintain. We know that colleges and universities will not easily abandon the commitment to general education of some sort, even if every decade sees a lessening of what they require. Insofar as career education is housed in such institutions, some modicum of liberal education will be required. Each institution will struggle to define the kind of liberal education or general education it considers suitable, and the range will undoubtedly reach from St. John's hundred "Great Books," to increased social and educational freedom, to the forms of general education suited to the modern world by experimental institutions. No general rule is or will be possible.

Finally, in the course of the disaggregation of many of the functions of higher education and as we move toward many specialized institutions and toward recurrent education (new forms of adult education taken at various times, for various purposes whether career, recreation, or personal information) one hopes that liberal education will remain as one option. In the disaggregation of higher education which we are now undergoing, and as we see new specialized forms of education developing for specific purposes, I suspect that general or liberal education will not lose out. We may not be very good any more at explicating its values or justifying its presence. And for this reason, we can make no rigid requirement that general education be taught everywhere and to every person. (That, in fact, would be an unrealistic demand when higher education has already been so broadly opened up.) But we can expect that, in a free market of choice, liberal or general education will survive and indeed may flourish. For even if we are confused in arguing for liberal or general education, it is hard to believe in a rapid decline in the appeal of what for so long has been considered the best, the most significant, and the most valuable *in itself*.

Notes

1. Lawrence Veysey, "Stability and Experiment in the American Undergraduate Curriculum," in Carl Kaysen, ed. *Content and Context.* New York: McGraw-Hill, 1973.
2. Joseph Tussman, *Experiment at Berkeley.* New York: Oxford University Press, 1969.
3. Daniel Bell, *The Reforming of General Education.* New York: Columbia University Press, 1966.
4. *Education at Berkeley.* Berkeley: University of California Press, 1966.
5. Walter Guzzardi, Jr., "The Uncertain Passage from College to Job." *Fortune,* January 1976, p. 168.

"Naught for Your Comfort"

HENRY C. JOHNSON, JR.

> I tell you naught for your comfort,
> Yea, naught for your desire,
> Save that the sky grows darker yet
> And the sea rises higher.
>
> G.K. Chesterton, *Ballad of the White Horse*

Nathan Glazer contributes an elegant demonstration of the futility of asking a contemporary social scientist what to *do* about a problem. He can tell us only how we got into the problem, why it could not have been otherwise, and why we can do nothing more about it now than we could have then. We can at best suffer that peculiarly human fate of being caught in the iron grip of inexorable events and doomed to realize it.

What could possibly justify such a tasteless accusation? In the first place, Professor Glazer not only does not lead us through the problem nor even to the problem. He leads us away from it. Facing the question of education beyond the economic model, he assumes that "beyond" means simply "in addition to." Stipulating that it is "hardly arguable" that the "main motor" of education has ever been anything but the economic, he proceeds to ask what "more" there could be. Moving from his initial consideration of the "broad term 'education,' " which he has summarily dismissed, Glazer invites us for a stroll through early American higher education and the various attempts to reform it. He concludes with a vintage sociological account of a quite specific phenomenon, the "general education movement." In pursuit of an explanation for the decline and apparent death of this particular "more" in education, Glazer poses three challenges that he believes cannot be met: the problem of definition, the problem of justification, and the problem of applying a concept of general education to the various levels and agencies characteristic of American schooling.

Although Professor Glazer has dismissed as impossible the task of defining the educational "more" that goes beyond an indisputable economic basis, he admits that at least the first two-thirds of the nineteenth century did have some grasp on the educational "more" we are trying to isolate. (I shall leave aside his assumption that contemporary education's economic orientation is not significantly different from that of earlier centuries. I cannot imagine what evidence would support such a contention.) As a curriculum it was, he says, "little more" than Greek, Latin, and mathematics; and it failed because it was wooden and unpalatable.

Such a curriculum would indeed have been wooden and unpalatable had it ever existed. But I find little in my acquaintance with the nineteenth century to justify such a caricature. Glazer seems to suggest that the languages alone were the curricular staple. But this is an egregious distortion. Most importantly, the curriculum embraced both the classical languages and the classical *literature*. It usually included rhetoric, mathematics, and, at least for the few who completed the curriculum, some sort of history as well. There were also "capstone courses" such as mental and moral philosophy, and a heavy component of scripture and theology—"subjects" absorbed both through the life of the college and its formal regimen. That few students attended and fewer still completed college work is important to keep in mind. In 1820, for example, no more that 9,400 souls, in a population approaching 10 million, completed something called "a bachelor's degree." Even as late as 1880, only 13 thousand baccalaureates were awarded in a nation of 50 million.

This curriculum doubtless could be wooden and unpalatable, at least in the more pedestrian institutions. Frequently the curriculum disregarded the practical urgencies of what would now be called "modernization"; and it was gradually becoming corrupted from within by a growing academic-vocational orientation. But it tried to be, and sometimes succeeded in being, a great deal more than Professor Glazer's account suggests.

Chiefly, it had attempted to emphasize two things: humane letters and mental discipline—with such other tools as might be necessary for life and learning. The humane letters conveyed not merely the skills of a trade but clear models of what it meant to be human (that is, what to say, what to value, and what to choose—in short, how to act as a man should act). Though we may dispute the psychological foundations upon which their selection rested, mathematics, the languages in their earlier stages, and the slowly ascendant sciences and practical subjects were thought both to be useful and to develop the art of thinking.

Professor Glazer rightly points out that the appearances were not saved by the introduction of the elective system. Indeed, Harvard and Mr. Eliot gave higher education the *coup de grace*, not because they were overly optimistic about the young or sought to provide excessive liberty, but rather because the elective system radically undermined the ground upon which any concept of education can be constructed. With the elective system, "education" (the term must carry quotation marks from the 1870s onward) became an increasingly private affair, related to individual interests and definable, if at all, only in private terms. The problem of curricular definition immediately became insuperable because the traditional concept of an education entailed the idea of some common set of beliefs and values and some notion of the common good. These are more than the sum of individual opinions and inclinations, and an educational foundation cannot be constructed from a mere aggregation of such interests.

Nor could the "general education movement," in part born of disenchantment with the social and political results of what had already become in a scant 50 years a thoroughly bureaucratized and industrialized "educational" enterprise, halt the decline. The attempt to maintain some concept of an education soon fell to the level of a pie-splitting contest euphemistically described as the setting of distribution requirements. But one can neither propose nor demand a common language in a Tower of Babel. Once the school has been redefined as an instrument for the achievement of essentially private goals, the effort appears arbitrary or even hypocritical. Neither tastes (as Cicero said) nor ambitions can be disputed. And, as Professor Glazer implies, if it cannot be done at Harvard or Berkeley, what chance is there for a Slippery Rock or Penn State?

Justifying any concept of general education is equally impossible. The undefinable is obviously unjustifiable. Professor Glazer is surely right here. Our justifications eventually did *become* economic and vocational. He also insists, however, that we could not and cannot "prove" that any education beyond the economic model would give us a better society, better men, or even a broader understanding of ourselves and our situation. Finally, Glazer insists, the application of any such further "educational matter," could it be defined and justified, is also impossible. We need not be concerned with what happens in the graduate school, since it does nothing more than build upon the college as the supposed locus of one's genuinely educational experience. But the college cannot succeed either because the secondary schools are no longer "strong and rigorous"—staffed as they are with college- and university-trained graduates. Furthermore, according to Professor Glazer, too many high school students are dropping out. Yet, if we connect high school experience with work in order to interest them, we only decrease the time necessary for general education. Our inevitable frustration is now complete: we cannot really educate anybody anymore so we might as well "disaggregate" the whole quixotic business. If we sunder the unity now archaically symbolized by our buildings and their comprehensive curricula, we will be free to pursue more responsive and economical modes of giving people what they want. We might even develop schools without pedagogical content for those who want only the socializing experience stripped of the tired rags of academia.

But of course Professor Glazer knows better than to leave us with such a counsel of despair. There are, he says, only two courses open to us in a "divided" and "pluralized" society. We may be many societies and have many cultures, but we are still one nation, and a nation has the right and the power to insist on something we might call "the study of citizenship." Since our city was fashioned in the eighteenth century, when the liberal studies were still in their prime, we have a legal warrant to insist that every citizen have "a knowledge of old matters." Thus, by the grace of history, everyone will have to study "matters" that place us squarely into "eighteenth-century language, thought, history, and philosophy." In addition to this "minimal" requirement, there will always be a few consumers, in a "free market of choice," who want much more, even as Glazer himself once did. And like the monasteries of early medieval Europe, a few institutions and programs will survive as repositories catering to this trade. Why? Because, says Professor Glazer, there really is a "best," a "most significant," and a "most valuable in itself," and it is simply "hard to believe" that it will disappear. So presumably when man comes once again to his senses and leaves the dark ages in which we now dwell for the light of the new renaissance, all will be there to be taken up once more.

Truly, Professor Glazer's conclusion is a masterful feat of academic legerdemain! Having dismissed the possibility of any meaningful education "beyond the economic model," he offers something in its place: the study of the oldest and the best. But the issue, as I have been trying to suggest, is not how, nor even whether, to revive either the traditional liberal arts or some paradigmatic general education program. The issue is whether we are to have anything resembling education at all for any but a small minority of our populace. The issue is whether we can any more really educate, rather than merely train, not only beauticians and cosmetologists but also physicians, ministers, and even college teachers—professions that once were almost inescapably humane and social but have themselves been reduced to disaggregated techniques and private interests. Although resolving this issue adequately would require extensive analysis, there are some considerations worth taking into account at this point.

Things were not better in the nineteenth century, as Professor Glazer does not need to be told. The glory of the nineteenth century was that, at least at first, it saw the problem. Its shame was that it turned away from it, not just educationally but socially and culturally as well. America entered the nineteenth century with the unshakable belief that if the new, self-governing society were to be more than just a legal fiction, it had an inescapable *educational* burden to bear. Horace Mann made all this clear: we shall, he said, either teach a voluntary compliance with "the laws of reason and duty" and through that process shape our own behavior, or we will necessarily be compelled to give involuntary compliance to the will of a lawgiver, and our only study in that case need be the content of his will. In other words, either we will make judgments and decisions for ourselves or they will be made for us. If we intend the former, its only possible basis is some set of commonly taught and accepted principles of belief and value. If we intend the latter, we need only learn to do as we are told. These are, Mann believed, the only alternatives, aside from the most unthinkable of all: an anarchy of private desires in which power becomes the only ordering principle.

It was no accident that Mr. Eliot, displaying that cat-like cultural agility which has kept Harvard in business these three centuries, shifted to education based on private interest almost precisely when the pursuit of the private became America's chief preoccupation. Though the old ideals continued to receive lip-service and exert a declining pragmatic power, the educational apparatus at every level quickly aligned itself with the new economy, the new world of work. It was a world of work which was itself rapidly entering a disintegration and privatization which no academic gloss could hide from critics like Veblen, Dewey, and Hutchins.

As I work through the nineteenth century and into the early twentieth, I am always struck by the clear transition from the supremacy of the *corporate,* within which one finds his part and gains his identity, through the still socially moral *individual* in debt to a larger whole to which he must render an account, and eventually to the new *private person* who sees nothing but his own interests and views society as but the servant to them.

Thus the issue that underlies not only education but society and work as well is whether we have anything we can legitimately hold and teach about social value. The new man, being produced in increasing quantities by almost every engine of this culture, thinks there is not. Firm in his lingering social-Darwinist faith, suffused with a naive technological optimism, and insulated from the issues by misapplications of the descriptive social and behavioral sciences, he feels quite free. And he is certain that the unbridled pursuit of his own interests cannot help but bring about the common good.

Dewey warned that we needed a new education, not only because of the discovery of new knowledge and the development of new social arrangements, but also because all of this would produce new problems. This new education, he said, would have to bridge the social, the economic, and the cultural. Its success would depend as much on contextual social and economic change as on narrowly pedagogical reform. Why? Because if education is inescapably linked to social experience, including work, and if that social experience becomes private and irrational, we shall necessarily witness the collapse of both the social and the educational.

We have never accepted Dewey's challenge. What is different about our present situation is that we can no longer ignore the problems of either education or work. We must have a new education beyond the economic model because the economic model we have adopted no longer furnishes us, if it ever did, with models for responsible social participation and adequate education. Neither striving to bring back general education nor affecting an olympian social-scientific detachment and relying on the survival of the finest will achieve what we must have.

Only a revolution in virtually all the areas of our experience will avoid the crisis. A mechanistic education, a mechanistic world of work, and a mechanistic social and behavioral science are, if you will, the co-conspirators who must be indicted forthwith if we are to avoid a cataclysm. The difficulty that besets us is not merely a problem in curriculum or method. Emptying human action of choice and value in favor of causal analyses and production techniques has emptied education of meaning. And meaningless education has in turn engendered the passivity, fatalism, and despair that vitiate not only democracy but humanity itself.

Education Beyond the Economic Model:
A Practitioner's View

HELEN D. WISE

In the last 200 years, our American concept of education has changed from the privilege of a few to a universal "right to learn." John Goodlad describes our public school concept as the "great American experiment in mass education," and all educators agree that, rightly or wrongly, no other country even attempts to educate its young as we do.

The problems we face in determining what education really is gain perspective when we look at the purpose of education as articulated by the 1970 White House Conference. While asserting that all American young people have the right to learn, the Conference asked and answered this question: "What would we have our citizen in the Twenty-first Century be?"

> We would have him be a man with a strong sense of himself and his own humanness, with awareness of his thoughts and feelings, with the capacity to feel and express love and joy and to recognize tragedy and feel grief. We would have him be a man who, with a strong and realistic sense of his own worth, is able to relate openly with others, to cooperate effectively with them toward common ends, and to view mankind as one while respecting diversity and difference. We would want him to be a being who, even while very young, somehow senses that he has it within himself to become more than he is now, that he has the capacity for lifetime spiritual and intellectual growth. We would want him to cherish that vision of the man he is capable of becoming and to cherish the development of the same potentiality in others.

(One is tempted to inquire whether he will be able to read and write too.)

This difference in expectations points up the major problem we face: we expect our schools to accomplish too much. Robert M. Hutchins noted that we too optimistically expect schools to be the "foundation of our freedom, the guarantee of our future, the cause of our prosperity and power, the bastion of our security, the bright and shining beacon that was the source of our enlightenment." Yet the severest criticism of public schools for the past 30 years has been that they have neither changed themselves nor reflected the changes in society.

But they *have* changed. First of all, many more young people finish school. In 1930, less than 30 percent were graduated from high school; in 1964, the percentage had risen to 65 percent. Eight of ten people 20 and 21 years old have at least a high school education; among people 30 to 34 years old, 69 percent have finished high school; among those 55 to 64 years old, 40 percent; and of those 75 years and older, only 24 percent.

"Yes," the critics answer, "they may be staying, but they aren't learning." So, secondly, it's important to note that students in elementary, junior high, and senior high schools did at least as well as, and in many cases better than, their counterparts in the schools of 19 of 20 other nations on achievement tests in science, reading comprehension, and literature. The latest testing involved 258,000 students in 9,700 schools. Moreover, researchers from the International Association for the Evaluation of Educational Achievement (based at Teachers College, Columbia University) point out that in evaluating any such study one should recognize that in the United States a relatively unselected group of students reaches the end of secondary education, while in most other countries, conscious selective processes operate to retain only the ablest students at the high school level.

This is, of course, the essence of the change in public schools in the twentieth century. We have always had children with disabilities, children who could not cope with the curriculum no matter how limited. But these children have not always had to perform efficiently in a highly technical society in which the labor of children has become suddenly superfluous. The schools have been extended to meet not the needs of the children necessarily, but the need of society to occupy them until they reach their majority. And we have demanded changes of these newly extended schools: in the '50s, we attacked them because they were deficient in the scholarly disciplines; in the '60s we found them joyless, insensitive, and unresponsive to the pupils and the communities.

As I ponder these charges, I can't help wondering about the joy in an early Pennsylvania schoolhouse with its mud floor and without heat or light. And I wonder about the mastery of academic disciplines there when I read that the average attendance for 126 14-year-old children in Central Pennsylvania in the early 1800s was 53 days.

We all remember the post-Sputnik decade when the schools were accused of failure because we had not produced the scientists to out-distance the Russians. But the schools responded. We studied science and matter and physics, and we put men on the moon. Incidentally, College Board scores show that the public schools of the 1960s did indeed accomplish their post-Sputnik mandate of producing students with higher mathematical, scientific, and technological skills. But once that happened, the schools were blamed for the dropouts and the increasing crime rate.

Yet the truth is that we have a better public education system than at any other time in our history. We have less illiteracy, more college graduates, and more human freedom and prosperity (even in the midst of a recession) than ever before. Our scientific accomplishments are unparalleled, and all of them can be traced to public education. Despite their shortcomings and the unreasonable demands placed upon them, our public schools have served us well. Moreover, they reflect the society in which they are found—the strengths, weaknesses, successes, and failures of each are reflected in the other.

What, then, do we look forward to in education? In the speech he intended to deliver on November 22, 1963, President Kennedy had written: "In a world of complex and continuing programs, in a world full of frustration and irritations, America's leadership must be guided by the lights of learning and reason—only an America which has fully educated its citizens is fully capable of tackling the complex problems and perceiving the hidden dangers of the world in which we live."

We must look again at the purpose of education. In recent years these purposes have been the material and social improvement of the individual and the establishment and maintenance of self-government in our community. Yet evidence has been growing that the whole idea of getting better jobs by earning more credentials is absurd: If one's object in going to school is to get ahead and one doesn't, why should one have gone? Why should others go?

Perhaps we should ask instead, as Robert Hutchins has, if there is any value left in Adam Smith's and John Stuart Mill's concern with the development of the individual as a human being, saved from stupidity, ignorance, and torpor. The individual—able to carry on a rational conversation and to use his mind which, too many feel, has been continually deteriorating as it concentrates on acquiring pieces of paper.

Werner Jaeger, in *Paideia,* maintained that education is the deliberate attempt to form ideal men. The aim of American education—specifically public education—was originally to form men as independent, self-governing members of a self-governing community. As technology has grown, our planet has shrunk. That community has become a world community. But unfortunately, American educational discussion omits such references and considers only the more selfish interests of neighborhoods, groups, or classes.

The doctrine of every man for himself loses its value or attraction in an interdependent world. And education is still the one institution that can help us preserve our common humanity. In addition, the creative and communicative arts have permanent relevance because they help the people of the world understand one another.

Mill said that education makes a man a more intelligent shoemaker, if that be his occupation, but not by teaching him how to make shoes; it does so by the mental exercises it gives and the habits it impresses. The advance of technology makes this observation more relevant now than it was one hundred years ago. As technology reduces the demand for skilled labor, it increases the need for intelligent citizens.

No economic system seems capable of fully keeping pace with the employment expectations of younger workers. There simply will not be enough good jobs for everyone who wants one and whose credentials say that he deserves one. There are three ways to respond: to change educational policies, to change the structure of work, or to change the economic system. But since we can't turn back the clock and close the colleges, no solution is really satisfactory. James O'Toole suggested that the most constructive thing education can do is to stop implicitly and explicitly selling education as an economic investment. He asks, "Are educational institutions to be the locus of the idealism so essential to a free society—or are they to become handmaidens of identity and economy?" In other words, can we really "gear all education to the world of work"?

Society must rid itself of the notion that the major purpose of education is to serve the economy and the economic needs of students. But we do need an integration of education and work. The separation of the two has been too much a part of American values. America has consistently maintained a dual faith—a faith in education, which has built our unique school system; and a basically anti-intellectual faith in experience. We have a crying need for flexibility and coordination. We see too much confusion about the role and purpose of career education. We should show genuine concern for the future of education beyond the economic model—education that is essential to the future of civilization.

Education Beyond the Economic Model: A View from Organized Labor

AL LORENTE

Professor Glazer places educational disciplines and curricula that make up "Education Beyond the Economic Model" into general and liberal education categories. As a representative of organized labor, and specifically of the United Auto Workers, I question this approach on the basis of our experience with the effects of insufficient and misdirected education acquired by the populace. Our views reflect sensitivities that come from representing working people. This representation often brings to light problems that originate far from the actual workplace.

The scope of U.A.W. activity includes educational matters as well as other matters of community interest. While engaging in external education projects that complement our internal educational activity, we have attempted to be innovative, creative, and effective. And much of our educational activity, both internal and external, reflects the U.A.W.'s conviction that public education must provide for more than merely conditioning a student (of any age) with an education from the so-called economic model.

Some Brief Historical Background
The current educational philosophy in labor as it relates to "Education Beyond the Economic Model" has evolved sequentially. This evolution can be traced (and has been traced by men like John A. Sessions and Gus Tyler) through the various documents of the American labor movement. Sessions, Assistant Director of Education of the AFL-CIO, and Tyler, Assistant President of the International Ladies Garment Workers' Union, amply demonstrate labor's concern in this area.[1]

Moreover, a resolution adopted in 1918 by the AFL bears a startling resemblance to the current career education publications coming from the United States Office of Education:

The true function of education is to develop personal powers and to give the individual control over himself so that he may have confidence in himself and may use his ability to the best advantage. The previous educational methods, which have not by any means been replaced by the newer ideals, dealt primarily with abstractions. That education dealt altogether with ideation. It ignored the daily experiences of the boy or girl, or man or woman. It appealed to that small percentage who desire truths for their own sake, to whom only the esoteric appeals. The ideals for the schools of the future, the movement for the new education which includes more than vocational and industrial education—it begins with the very fundamentals of mental training. This education begins with those things which appeal to the child and arouse his curiosity in the daily life, the actual material things with which he comes in contact. These things the schools of the future are to explain to the child in order that he may have full and complete understanding of his daily life and thereby be master of himself and his environment because he knows how to coordinate his own powers. Flowers, fruits, animals, pieces of furniture are all marvelous and wonderful objects to the child; they appeal to his curiosity; they stir him because they are real. These should be the first things with which education deals; abstractions should be introduced in connection with realities.

Current and Contemporary Activity

The Education Department of the U.A.W.'s International Union, supported by dues money, maintains the largest union education staff in America's labor movement, with education representatives in each of our 18 regions. An examination of the U.A.W.'s educational activity reveals a commitment to pushing public education well beyond the economic model. In a speech delivered before the American Association of Community and Junior Colleges in April of 1975, President Leonard Woodcock had this to say:

> We are convinced that it will be a scandal . . . if the community colleges and the American labor movement fail to enter into . . . partnership to provide American workers a relevant education not only for the world of work but to deliver as well the knowledge and insight essential in broadening life's horizons and improving the quality of citizenship.
>
> Certainly we both recognize the social value of an educated citizenry and the worth of the individual. We both favor equality of opportunity and social and economic mobility.
>
> From our own experience, we know that community colleges have a varied, flexible curriculum, an obvious essential for lifelong learning in a rapidly changing society and economy.

The U.A.W.'s sensitivity to the strengths and weaknesses of the public education process comes about in several ways. Two of the predominant experiences that can lead to this sensitivity are experiences as users of the products of public education and experiences as a prime contractor for millions of dollars worth of manpower training money.

As users of the products of public education, we have seen surface many problems caused by inadequate and inferior education. Difficulties encountered by management because of poorly educated employees quickly become the problems of the collective bargaining affiliates representing those employees. This is probably the single best reason that views concerning the faults of public education are similar (though not identical) whether they come from business and industry or from organized labor.

Since 1966, the U.A.W. has received more than 15 million dollars from the Department of Labor and the Department of Health, Education and Welfare to conduct manpower training programs in many different cities across the country. While operating these programs, we often enroll at a remedial level high school graduates fresh from commencement. We find ourselves teaching them how to read, write, reason, and perform basic math.

While a good part of this effort goes to enhance a person's employability, extensive counseling activities attempt to provide an increased awareness of family, citizenship, and personal responsibility. One can see why these experiences make us sensitive to the faults in the public education processes.

We believe that these faults lie with the system rather than with the people involved in that system. In our travels around the country, we meet many fine educators keenly aware of the faults and trying to correct them. Entrenchment of tradition, the guarding of proprietary interests, and the lack of an all-out, well coordinated effort involving all segments of our communities are some of the reasons why public education has not responded to the fundamental educational needs of our society.

The U.A.W. has recently begun to participate in the career education movement currently in progress. And one of the products of our cooperation with the Michigan Career Education Advisory Commission has been a policy statement, issued January 1976, forthrightly addressing the topic of "Education Beyond the Economic Model":

1. Career education is a response to the call for educational reform of a system which has failed to respond viably to the educational needs of today's society. The U.A.W., along with other labor organizations, participated in the development of this reform.

2. The U.A.W. views a person's career as his or her whole lifetime, which includes the various life roles experienced by our populace. With little exception, all persons will be students, family members, and citizens, as well as workers. Career education relates to each of these life roles. Students must learn how to learn. This will provide the adaptability competencies necessitated by changing job conditions. Current statistics indicate the average person will change jobs some six times during a lifetime. New skills may be required along with refurbishing of old talents.

3. While part of the concept of career education provides that education should be preparation for work, the entire concept also stresses that public education must accomplish other things. Even though work is an important aspect of one's career, it does not represent the totality of a lifetime. Cultural, aesthetic, and leisure-time activities must be considered. Earning a living is not the same as living a rich and rewarding life. The skills required to understand and cope with the problems of our culture and society must also be taught, as well as the skills to bring about those constructive changes a viable society constantly needs.

4. Career education is expected to create a citizen who is self-confident and culturally advanced; one who relates well to others, adapts to change, possesses both living skills and job skills, and who can manage the tools of his or her occupation. The U.A.W. endorses the career education philosophy, and is willing to work with educators and others toward its successful implementation.

A consensus within the career education movement is emerging. In October of 1975, General Motors announced its support of the movement. "Career education," its policy statement said, "is intended to provide students of all ages necessary information and developmental experiences to prepare them for living and working. Preparation for work is a major goal but not the only goal of career education, since work does not exist in isolation from all other aspects of life."

Cross-sectional support for "Education beyond the Economic Model" is inherent in the current career education activity. Stephen Bailey, Vice President of the American Council of Education, traces recent developments from "the bad-mouthing of baccalaureate liberal learning" to "the glory of American higher education in its pluralism" and concludes that "what is needed now is a constructive partnership to bring about education concepts that are technologically sophisticated and humanistically informed."[2]

As Willard Wirtz wrote in *The Boundless Resource,*

> An education work policy is not one that misconceives of education as having as its purpose the preparation of people for work. Rather, it includes this purpose as part of education's function of preparing people for life, of which work is one part; it takes full account of learning as a human value in itself.
>
> And further, to identify the human resource as an essential ingredient of systematic growth is in no way to confuse the priorities of individual and institutional interests. The superior claim on reason of this different growth concept is that to develop people's capacities more fully inevitably increases their prospects for a higher, better, and more satisfying life experience.[3]

The U.A.W. subscribes to Wirtz's view.

Conclusions

Professor Glazer's reference to "the current disaggregation of higher education" as being "a form of salvation for general and liberal education" (the category where he places "Education Beyond the Economic Model") lacks the specificity implied by the current call for educational reform. This call is being answered by many who have joined Bailey's "constructive partnership." The partners are coming from primary, secondary, and higher education as well as from business and industry.

We representatives of organized labor see members of society as total human beings. This recognition demands that we make concerted efforts to improve the quantity and quality of the education given to our members, their families, and others in the American community. The educational experiences of students of all ages should relate closely and clearly to living experiences. Learning how to learn (that is, the development of decision-making, adaptability, and coping skills) is a proper function of public education. While job preparation is important, cultural, aesthetic, and leisure activities are too. Insofar as "Education beyond the Economic Model" provides for these experiences, and provides them for a broad spectrum of our people, it should always be an integral part of educational planning.

Notes

1. John A. Sessions. "The History of Labor's Pursuit of Education (1800–1935)." Unpublished paper prepared for the Education Department of the AFL-CIO, 1975; and Gus Tyler, "What Kind of Career Education?" Unpublished paper, 1973.
2. Stephen K. Bailey. "Career Education and Higher Education." Paper presented to the National Institutes of Education Conference, George Washington University, Washington, D.C., 1973.
3. Willard K. Wirtz. *The Boundless Resource.* Washington: New Republic, 1975.

V
Occupational Curricula and "Generalizable" Education

Occupational Curricula and "Generalizable" Education

THOMAS F. POWERS

Anyone who addresses the subject of occupational curricula finds at least two distinct audiences, each with its own point of view. For one audience, the terms "vocational" and "vocational education" have very specific meanings tied to vocational education legislation and funding. The second group considers the term "vocational education" more generally, as more or less synonymous with "occupational education" or "educating for careers."

I am convinced that vocational education—as defined in the acts—is simply part of the broader phenomenon of occupationally oriented education—that is, educating for careers. This overt occupational concern in education seems to be increasing rapidly at all levels. Thus what we are dealing with is important to all educators; a parochial view will not suffice. This vocational content (in the broader sense) occasions concern and suspicion among many educators—but it is a fact of life.

Another important term, "general education," may have different meanings for different readers. For one group, this term describes a program of general studies in a comprehensive high school for students who are not college bound. To vocational educators, general education is "what we've been trying to get away from," and what Huff calls in an earlier chapter "the real bottom track." To the other group, however, "general education" conjures up Daniel Bell's *The Reforming of General Education* or the landmark *General Education in a Free Society.* There is sufficient criticism of general education from its own supporters to indicate the difficulty of succeeding in the ambitious endeavor which is general education positively conceived, and Professor Glazer has indicated some of the reasons why this is so. Among my readers, I suspect one group of educators feels very strongly that a free society must attempt to achieve general education, while another sees general education as a model of mass education that has been tried and has failed.

While I can cheerfully abandon the term "general education" in deference to the meaning vocational educators attach to it, it is clear that the goals of general education, which I'll call "generalizable education," must be an integral part of vocational curricula in this rapidly changing society of ours if only to serve the students' vocational interests.

Elsewhere in this volume the philosophical and economic arguments against a narrow "skills" focus for occupational curricula have been made, A number of writers, however, have alluded to the "use" of a skills focus to motivate students to learn what might otherwise not interest them. Clearly, then, one problem in curriculum planning is how to use the student's occupational interest to structure the learning of important general skills so as to achieve the learning necessary both for work on the job and work and play in the many other roles that make up what Dewey called a vocation in its fullest sense.

In the next part of this paper I will describe one model, in use in food service education at the secondary level, which addresses this problem and achieves what I've called generalizable education.

A related problem is the identification of the elements of a knowledge base appropriate to the field of work the student is interested in. There is more to the occupational content of the occupational curriculum than just a sugar coating to make a general education palatable. We make this implicit contract with our students: "If you study these courses, you will improve your chances of getting a job and advancing in it." In order to fulfill this contract for "curricular usefulness," we must accept and deal with the problems in the world of work posed by rapidly changing social, technical, and economic environments, as well as the challenge these changes present in preparing students for a lifetime of meaningful work. In a later part of this paper I will discuss a strategy used by one industry-related program to develop a model of the future of an industry in order to provide general guidelines for curriculum planning.

An important means of relating the curriculum to what is actually happening in an occupation is the field experience. A difficulty with field experiences, however, is that they generally separate the practical from the theoretical rather than integrating them. In the concluding section of this paper, I will describe how the practical and the theoretical aspects of field experiences have been integrated in an associate degree curriculum in Hotel and Food Service Management.

Generalizing the Occupational Curriculum

Recent national evaluation studies of traditional vocational programs present numerous negative findings. Many students, they report, earn higher wages by leaving their field of training at the time of graduation, and more than half the graduates take jobs in fields completely unrelated to their high school vocational training. Another disturbing finding is that a large proportion of vocational education graduates remain in unskilled and semiskilled jobs three years after graduation. These national studies, moreover, found no difference between vocational and academic graduates in' unemployment rates (6).* In an earlier section, Lewis suggested that final vocational planning at this high school level is inappropriate.

Another recent study supports the notion that students' personality development needs are not well served by either of the two current vo-tech logistical tactics: the separate vocational high school or the busing to a part-time vo-tech school from a "home school." This study concluded that "comprehensive high schools seemed the most viable administrative configuration for servicing the diverse needs of today's high school students" (7).

These studies do not "disprove" the validity of secondary vocational education. They do argue, however, for more flexible vocational education models that use the student's vocational motivation to supply the rationale for learning. Such education aims to combine many of the positive goals of general education within a vocational context in which preparation for life includes preparation for work. As Jerome Ziegler recently said, "Any subject, liberal or technical, can be a window to the world if well taught" (8).

Too often occupational curricula teach the solutions to problems rather than *problem-solving*. A curriculum that presents *solutions* commits itself to narrow skill training—and skills change too rapidly for that approach. Courses can and must present factual material related to a field of work. But they should be constructed to take maximum advantage of their potential for generalizability. In a society changing as rapidly as ours, solutions served up by the dead hand of the past are frequently out-of-date by the time a student is ready to put them into practice. An alternative strategy suggests the development of a problem-solving approach in occupational curricula which implicitly incorporates the kinds of

---

*Numbers in parentheses refer to References at the end of this essay.

learning objectives I call generalizable education into occupational preparation.

I recently visited one secondary school food service education project that has successfully attained the goals of generalizable education through the medium of occupational instruction in a comprehensive high school.

Project FEAST—Food Education and Service Training—was begun in California by Hilda Watson Gifford under grants from the Ford Foundation and the Office of Education. I had an opportunity to observe an offshoot of this project that has taken root in the state of Washington. I talked there with students, teachers, and school administrators involved in Project FEAST and came away feeling that I had seen the theory of career education put into practice. I might note that Project FEAST is really not a curriculum but rather an instructional system, a team approach to teaching what is—for the most part—the same subject matter presented in any comprehensive high school curriculum but taught through the medium of food service.

First of all, the team is led by a home economist as team captain, and central to Project FEAST is the foods lab normally associated with a comprehensive high school home economics foods course. Working with the home economist is an English teacher, a math or business education teacher, and a guidance counselor. The fifth member of the team is the school's food service manager.

Let me give some examples of how FEAST works. In an English class I visited I heard the instructor play tapes of food service radio commercials. Students were instructed to identify the "strong" verbs, the "strong" adjectives, and the "strong" adverbs. Another assignment, I learned, would involve writing commercials. Students also undertake a project that requires them to design a restaurant as a team project and to present the results both orally and in written reports. The presentation of a recipe to be prepared by the class becomes the occasion for a demonstration speech. Students can see that what they are doing is related to their future interests, and that encourages them to learn. Thus FEAST provides a course in communication, both written and oral, involving not only the act of communicating but also the act of comprehending communication.

The FEAST math course relies on such activities as converting small quantity recipes to larger quantities, computing the school lunch storeroom inventory, and payroll computation—all of these exercises with a purpose the student can grasp. As one teacher explained it to me, "math *is* management. It's the math that you need to make a profit."

Of course, the foods course in the home ec lab lies at the center of the experience. Much of the work in the English and math courses is related to what happens in the lab. The lab is very highly project-oriented. Projects involve running a specialized restaurant for a few days; providing a small bake shop whose output is sold to students and teachers in the school; and serving special occasion banquets for students, faculty members, school board members, or community leaders. Students take turns serving as managers and supervisors, as well as workers. For me, the most important and interesting thing about these lab projects is that management preparation is carried out successfully at the high school level.

Jencks and Riesman tellingly criticize higher education's emphasis on abstract reasoning and verbal skills, which are of paramount importance to only a small portion of tomorrow's workers. They suggest that large organizations

> desperately need managers who can keep a large number of diverse personalities working in harmony. . . . One reason such managers are in such short supply is that the high school senior who is good at getting people to do what he wants and at keeping them from getting at each other's throats cannot get through college on that account. . . . [O]ne could therefore argue that America needed colleges where personal skills of this sort were valued more than verbal facility and where students of this sort consequently felt comfortable and competent. (9)

The point Jencks and Riesman make regarding college can be applied as well to much of secondary education. The student who lacks the traditional academic skills, yet has abilities which *are* needed in our society, experiences humiliation in an academic context where his skills are not valued. On the other hand, Project FEAST, and the Seminar-Practicum to be discussed shortly, not only recognize and reinforce these important skills, but also teach students a good bit about the nonacademic behaviors characteristic of the successful leaders at all levels in our society.

The evidence I offer here is anecdotal rather than statistical. Moreover, one must visit Project FEAST and talk to the students to appreciate its effectiveness fully. But I remember asking a student to explain how the class worked, what his role as manager was, and how he liked the course. Clearly, he was excited about the subject matter. He found it interesting and he could see *why* he was doing what he was doing. Then he said, "Another good thing is that you're not getting behind in your school work. You get your English and your math." In short, here was a vocational student who did not feel left out of the academic process.

Again and again, I met students enthusiastic about and committed to what they were doing in spite of the fact that nearly all of them had been guided into Project FEAST because they had academic deficiencies. Again and again, instructors pointed out that Project FEAST represented the first academic success these students had had.

One incident stands out in my mind. By prior arrangement, I visited an English instructor in class. She gave the students some busy work and began to talk with me. But that proved impossible. The students kept interrupting us politely and courteously with questions, all of which, however, related to the class's work. At first I thought the interruptions would quickly cease. But they didn't, and gradually both the instructor and I realized that the students were simply not going to let some bearded professor take *their* teacher away from *them*. We finally gave up trying to talk, and I stood back observing with great interest a class in high school English composed of so-called poorer students earnestly pursuing the English language through the medium of food service commercials. How many English classes are there in America's high schools that would not *welcome* an opportunity to goof off for a few minutes while their teacher talked to a visitor?

Another instance stands out. I mentioned to an instructor how interested and active all his students were. He replied that one key to FEAST was its voluntary nature. No one was forced to take FEAST. "If a student isn't doing his work," he said, "you can always say, 'If you're not here to learn, maybe you don't belong here.'" Clearly, the fact that students wanted to participate in their education was crucial to their success. In fact, a very substantial portion of these problem students are discovering through Project FEAST that they *can* learn. A surprising number go on to two- or four-year colleges.

I asked FEAST's administrators if they thought the instructional system had a more general application—that is, could be used as a model for the development of similar programs in other fields. They agreed that it could, and they mentioned, specifically, programs in the medical occupations, child care, and clothing studies. The list could undoubtedly be lengthened.

In fact, the lists of successful career programs recounted by, among others, Goldhammer, Somers, and Little, is a long one (10, 11). Indeed, the whole notion of career education isn't new. Its model appeared in the 1906 Commonwealth of Massachusetts "Report of the Committee on Industrial and Technical Education" (12). Why, then, is it that education has been so slow to adopt a model whose good sense appeals to the intuition and which has been around since the turn of the century? The answer, I suggest, is clear. Progress has been stifled by an unreasoning and unreasonable prejudice against occupational education in the educational establishment and a reluctance among vocational educators to adopt or adapt more dynamic models for achieving their ends.

Developing a View of the Future

The difficulties of basing vocational programs on detailed manpower planning models are legion, as Thurow and Herr have amply demonstrated in an earlier section. Indeed, crystal ball gazing has long been recognized as a difficult art. For curricula that claim to prepare for the world of work, however, some view of the future is essential because students will not typically hit their occupational or professional stride until some five or ten years after graduation.

Thurow suggests that the principal job of occupational curricula should be to gain students' entry into internal labor markets with their opportunities for continuing training and education. We need not, however, assume that the content of the occupational curriculum will have only that utility. Properly constructed, an occupational curriculum will identify a knowledge base that can be useful to a knowledge worker for much or all of his or her working life. Clearly, however, to achieve that goal the curriculum's approach to the knowledge base must be dynamic, not backward looking.

With funding from the Research Coordinating Unit for Vocational Education of the Pennsylvania Department of Education, Penn State's Food Service and Housing Administration Program recently concluded a two-year interdisciplinary study of the future of the food service industry (2–5). This study involved a team that included economists, food scientists, and nutritionists, as well as engineers, an urban planner, and social and clinical psychologists. The study attempted to develop both numerical scenarios of manpower demand in the food service industry and a qualitative view of the kinds of roles that would be included within those numerical forecasts. The study presents some interesting conclusions, none of which needs to be viewed as a precise point estimate to have general, suggestive meaning. And the work offers a useful case study, illustrating one constructive attempt to relate occupational curricula at several levels to emerging industry trends.

To begin with, while the Bureau of Labor Statistics projects an increase of 22 percent in the work force from 1972 to 1985, our studies suggest that the demand for food service workers will increase by about 62 percent in the same period. This leads us to several conclusions. First, the demand for workers in this area clearly indicates plenty of employment opportunities for food service graduates and so an implicit contract regarding employment is probably justifiable. One of the problems of secondary food service education programs, however, is that the majority of graduates enter semiskilled or unskilled positions which, traditionally, have not paid well. A second conclusion of our study is that the wage level for these positions in the industry will increase more rapidly than wage levels in the economy in general because of the very substantial demand for food service workers compared to the increase in supply that a normal work force growth would bring about.

Perhaps even more interesting than the aggregate growth in food service manpower is our projection that, while the traditional skilled and semiskilled roles in the industry will grow about 45 percent in the period projected, the number of unskilled workers will grow approximately 80 percent and managers (including supervisors) about 90 percent. These divergent trends within the total food service work force clearly have curricular implications. At one level, they suggest that developing the means of socializing slower students to gainful employment would be functional. On the other hand, they underscore the usefulness of management preparation at all levels of the educational system.

Another major conclusion we reached was that the trend toward simplification of food service operations will continue, abetted by the trend toward fast food and quasi-fast food operations, by the centralization of food service systems, and by the growing mechanization of food preparation. This trend helps explain the need for more unskilled workers. In effect, it is a late continuation of a trend in the service industries that the manufacturing economy underwent in the industrial revolution, a move toward the rationalization of production and away from social institutions based on the artisan.

A fourth major trend is the increasing significance of the dining scene as experience. The restaurant, as opposed to the inn, dates back only to the eighteenth century. Restaurants take their name from a soup served to travelers, *ristorante*, which meant literally "restorative." In a hectic world it is not surprising that a social restorative function, entertainment in ambience, is receiving renewed emphasis. In terms of labor demand, we feel that this trend will necessitate more and better servers. Thus, increasing attention to offering secondary students preparation for roles as waitresses and waiters is justified. Income data indicate that at the upper end of their scale servers earn $20,000 and more a year.

With the help of social and clinical psychologists we gradually developed the view that a server's skills go beyond the purely mechanical and enter the realm of interpersonal skills. Mechanical serving skills are not unimportant, but they are not, by themselves, sufficient to develop behavior that will earn social and economic rewards for future servers. For this reason, we have begun to develop a new approach to server training based on the model of interpersonal skill training developed by Danish (13) that prepares students for the economically more rewarding roles we see already developing in the service area. While the design of these waiter/waitress preparation experiences was initially intended for secondary vocational school programs, we are also experimenting with the adaptation of the interpersonal skill training model to associate and baccalaureate management-oriented programs to prepare managers for what will clearly be a more "client-centered" food service industry.

Another major development likely to emerge in food service involves such government programs as school lunch and congregate feeding. Our projections suggest that this area will grow between two and three times as rapidly as food service in general. Government food service programs are likely to fit the manpower model already mentioned in that roles will be predominantly either unskilled or managerial and supervisory. In thinking about the unskilled workers in these programs, it is useful to recall that many secondary food service education students come from the group called slow learners. The relatively stable employment patterns in government agencies appear to offer reasonable employment opportunities for these students. On the other hand, because the major growth of government food service will be in new programs rather than in established school food service, the government sector will need a new cadre of managers and supervisors. Accordingly, students qualified for these management roles would be in a position to enter major new organizations on the ground floor in a period of growth. We have identified a number of areas of particular importance to future government food service employees, such as applied nutrition, as a necessary part of the curriculum.

The study of the future of food service was used in developing secondary school curriculum guidelines as well as in considering two- and four-year college curricula. Our manpower projections suggest that the traditional skilled and semiskilled roles will be growing at about twice the rate of the work force in general. The very rapid growth in the demand for unskilled workers, moreover, is likely to coincide with that portion of the secondary school students in food service programs who are the slow learners. Thus we raise the question, What can usefully be taught to people whose roles are likely to be unskilled? One answer comes to us from both secondary food service teachers and industry leaders with whom we worked. They told us it would be most useful if we could "teach the work ethic." It would be a real service to the industry, and to the students, if we could, for instance, teach them simply the importance of coming to work. Given this body of students as a target population, we have begun to develop gaming strategies that permit students to play the various roles found in food service and to develop some subjective identification with those roles. By gaming, we hope the students will gain some understanding of the various roles in a food service system. The games operate in the affective as well as the cognitive domain, so that a student can "feel" that the work ethic is really a practical social institution and a useful way of relating people to one another in work settings.

A second element of the curriculum we hope to develop for this particular clientele involves the interpersonal skill training referred to earlier. We know that the largely unskilled roles emerging in government food service programs are unskilled only from a culinary standpoint. In government food service, and particularly in the most rapidly growing preschool and congregate feeding programs, employees deal with people who are at special states in the life cycle which need and merit specialized attention—either the very young or the very old. While culinary skills may not be essential to this work, interpersonal skills responsive to the aging or the very young are essential. In fact, they not only accommodate the client, but also heighten the employee's own enjoyment of the work. Most food service employees will verify that the greatest enjoyment in their work comes with pleasing the guest or client. Thus interpersonal skill training in the school constitutes a job enrichment strategy, a way of turning the routine into the rewarding by providing unique skills.

The intense demand forecasted for managers supports the continuing growth of two-year and four-year college programs in this field. It suggests, too, the crucial need for articulation between secondary school vocational programs and two- and four-year institutions. The potential for applying the study to associate and baccalaureate degree programs is extensive, but perhaps an example will suffice. The growth in centralized food service systems is extremely important for curriculum planning in post-secondary hospitality education. Centralized systems require simpler work roles but more demanding management activities. While the generalist food service manager may serve the basic need of the industry for the foreseeable future, specialized skills in such areas as industrial engineering and operations research will have to enter more prominently into associate and baccalaureate curricula.

We don't feel we have any precise point estimates. But we do feel that the guidance this effort provided was immensely useful. Some of the ways our study changed the way we think about the curriculum are outlined in the accompanying table. Similar studies in other fields would, I suspect, have real value for both faculty and students.

The Field Experience

Field experiences are often cited by occupational educators as one of the key elements in an occupational curriculum. President Knowles of Northeastern University has supplied a traditional definition of cooperative education:

1. The student's off-campus experience should be related as closely as possible to his field of study and individual interest within the field.

2. The employment must be a regular, continuing, and essential element in the educational process.

3. Some minimum amount of employment and minimum standard of performance must be included in the requirement for the degree or certificate presented by the school.

4. The working experience ideally should increase in difficulty and responsibility as the student progresses through the academic curriculum. (14)

Field experiences have been helpful in reaching the large number of people from lower socioeconomic groups now entering higher education (15). Knowles points out, however, the considerable difficulty in evaluating off-campus experiences. For example, there is the lack of real control over the off-campus learning environment by

Some Conclusions from the Study of the Food Service World of Work

Projected Change	Percentage	Implications for World of Work	Implications for Curriculum Planning
Work force (1972–85)			
Total work force growth	22	Rising wages	
Food service work force growth	62		
Traditional roles increase	45	Continuing solid demand for skilled and semiskilled workers	Continuing emphasis on culinary and operational skill preparation
Unskilled roles increase	80	Industrial revolution escalates in the food service industry	Interpersonal skill training; work ethic gaming strategies
Management and supervisory roles increase	90	same	Modular strategy; Emphasis on articulation
Industry organization and operation			
Continuing and accelerating simplification and centralization of food service system		Reinforces trend toward greater need for unskilled and management employees	Work ethic gaming strategies; Modular strategy; Emphasis on articulation; Post-secondary: increased emphasis on operations research and industrial engineering
Increasing significance of government food service		same	Interpersonal skill training for prospective workers in preschool and congregate feeding programs
Increasing significance of dining as an entertainment experience		Increasing demand for servers	Waiter/waitress training redeveloped in terms of interpersonal skill training

the academic faculty. And coupled with this lack of control is the lack of a coherent design in what the student learns (16). Moreover, the unstructured field experience separates the practical and the theoretical. Dewey tells us that experience is effective if the student realizes "the place of the particular . . . truth he is dealing with in carrying to fruition the act with which he is concerned" (1). But the unstructured field experience seems to signal a student that theory and practice are somehow in different worlds. This reinforcing of the separation of the practical from the theoretical is precisely what led Dewey and other students of the educational process to abhor a narrow skill-related approach. Thus a field experience system that fuses the practical and theoretical has much to recommend it.

The Food Service and Housing Administration program at Penn State, under funding from the Research Coordinating Unit for Vocational Education of the Pennsylvania Department of Education and the U.S. Public Health Service, undertook to redevelop its associate degree program around a controlled field experience we call the Seminar-Practicum (17). The Seminar Practicum relies on a triad of learning experiences—field, text, and class—to fuse the practical and theoretical. The Seminar-Practicum has allowed us to bring the real world into a classroom. Moreover, it forces a student to see the real connection between classroom theory and field practices by using the field to inculcate some of the theoretical and factual content of the curriculum.

The first element in this instructional system requires second-year students to hold a paying part-time job in the field for a minimum of 15 hours per week throughout that year. Finding part-time employment in the food service industry has proven to be no problem around the Reading, Pennsylvania, area where our associate degree program is located.

The second element in the instructional system involves a series of specialized instructional modules that direct the students' attention to appropriate problems in the work place and supplement the learning available from the field experience.

The third element in the system is a weekly three-hour seminar in which the real world of the field experience and the theoretical world of the text confront one another in class discussion. Students raise questions about practices they encounter that vary from the text, and they compare experiences in various establishments. Thus they gain not only from their own field experience but, in large part, from the field experiences of the other students. The student who is accustomed to the traditional lecture and exam model may be frustrated by the Seminar-Practicum at first because he is required to study somewhat independently, to make critical judgments, and to fend for himself in the field. Since this is a three-term experience, however, the process is dynamic and the student gradually becomes more comfortable directing his own study and work. As one of our instructors said,

> As the terms went by, I found our students using their own resources to gather information more and more frequently; and I found them relying on their text materials and on me less and less. When I mentioned that they had begun to solve their own problems maturely in the forbidding real world setting, most of them would shrug it off as if it were the most natural thing in the world. (18)

Evaluation of the cognitive learning suggests that our students secure a solid mastery of both the theoretical and the practical aspects of the subject matter covered in the Seminar-Practicum and are satisfied with their learning experience. Formal evaluation and continuing experience also reveal strong industry and community support for the system.

Since this instructional system is partly a substitute for the old, expensive laboratory experience, it offers the institution definite time, space, and capital economies. Moreover, since the student must be employed for wages as a requirement of the course, it also reduces the net cost of his education.

The Seminar-Practicum avoids making abstract and complex what is best taught in a concrete, down-to-earth way. And, to repeat, it dramatizes for a student the connection between mental effort and work done in the real world.

We believe the Seminar-Practicum to be an instructional model that has potential uses in many other fields. We first developed it to teach food production and management skills. We have subsequently adapted it to teach normal diet modification to dietetic technicians in a nutrition course and management skills to hotel and food service students, and it undoubtedly has applications in other fields as well. But most important, like few other field experiences, the Seminar-Practicum fuses theory and practice and brings the real world into the classroom.

Conclusion

This essay is intended to give support to three basic conclusions. First, it is clear that a curriculum design can be achieved which takes advantage of the student's current interests to teach both job-related and more general intellectual skills.

Second, while detailed views of the future manpower demand are clearly suspect, some grasp of the qualitative and quantitative demand can be developed by a careful study of trends in a field of work, and this grasp can inform curriculum planning in useful ways. Clearly the occupational content of occupational curricula need not be simply a sugar-coating to disguise general education. Instead, that curriculum can encompass a knowledge base appropriate to beginning a life's work and be useful in more than simply gaining entry into the crucially important internal labor markets.

Third, field experiences need not be viewed as "practical" and hence separate from "theoretical." Indeed, occupational programs, through the Seminar-Practicum and similar models, can lead the way for education generally to fuse the intellectual and practical in a meaningful and demanding way.

Finally, I hope this paper offers not only support for these contentions but also examples suggestive of action.

References

1. John Dewey. *Democracy and Education*. New York: Free Press, 1966, p. 306.
2. Thomas F. Powers, ed. *The Future of Food Service: A Basis for Planning*. University Park, Pa.: Service Management Reports, 1974.
3. Thomas F. Powers. *The Future of Food Service, 1985–1990*. University Park, Pa.: Service Management Reports, 1975.
4. Thomas F. Powers, ed. *Centralized Food Service Systems*. University Park, Pa.: Service Management Reports, 1975.
5. Thomas F. Powers, ed. *Technical Papers on the Future of the Food Service Industry*. University Park, Pa.: Service Management Reports, 1975.
6. Anon. *Work in America*. Cambridge, Mass.: MIT Press, n.d., pp. 138–40.
7. Clarence A. Dittenhafer, "Students' Perceptions of Personality Needs and Environmental Press as a Function of Program Separation." *Journal of Vocational Education* 4 (1974): 155–72.
8. Jerome M. Ziegler, "Some Questions Before Us: Notes Toward the Future of Higher Education." *Daedalus* 2 (Winter 1975): 210–21.
9. Christopher Jencks and David Riesman. *The Academic Revolution*. New York: Anchor Books, 1968, p. 143.
10. Keith Goldhammer and Robert E. Taylor, eds. *Career Education: Perspective and Promise*. Columbus, Ohio: Merrill, 1972, pp. 33–62.

11. Gerald G. Somers and J. Kenneth Little. *Vocational Education: Today and Tomorrow.* Madison: University of Wisconsin Center for Studies in Vocational and Technical Education, 1971, passim.

12. Arthur G. Wirth. *Education in the Technological Society: The Vocational-Liberal Studies Controversy in the Early Twentieth Century.* New York: Intext, 1972, p. 79.

13. Steven J. Danish and A.L. Hauer. *Helping Skills: A Basic Training Program.* New York: Behavioral Publications, 1973.

14. Asa S. Knowles. "Cooperative Education: The Catalyst for Innovation and Relevance." *Daedalus* 2 (Fall 1975): 202–9.

15. Peter H. Bingen. "Education in the World of Work." *Change,* February 1973, pp. 35–37.

16. Joseph Koppel. "The Field Experience in HRI Education." *Journal of Hospitality Education,* July 1976.

17. Thomas F. Powers, ed. *The Seminar-Practicum: A Community Based Instructional System for Paraprofessional Education.* University Park, Pa.: Service Management Reports, 1974, pp. 17–37 and 91–149.

18. James B. Hicks. "Application of a Self-Instructional System for Paraprofessional Education in Home Economics" in Powers, ibid., p. 72.

The Occupational Curriculum as a Problem in Design

WILLIAM E. TOOMBS

My remarks emphasize the education side of the phrase "occupational education." They are directed at two concepts introduced by Dr. Powers' paper: the idea of "generalizable education" and the "contract for usefulness."

One of the challenging features of education as a profession is that practitioners are constantly pressed toward a consideration of essentials. Sometimes the press comes from students who raise embarrassing questions about where ideas come from. Sometimes the reconsideration is forced by skeptical and occasionally irritated laymen. In times of rapid change, the press can come from the society in which the educational enterprise is set. For example, a few years ago the fiscal matters in higher education—program budgeting, long-range financial planning, systematic information gathering, linear programming, and management technology in other forms—enjoyed great attention. They were all discussed as though all factors in the educational equation were known and as if most of these factors were manageable. Extramural elements in the system, like legislators and coordinating boards, were considered casually, if at all.

Since those early years of the decade, inflation has destroyed any illusion that the fiscal destiny of education was under complete control. Thus we have been driven to face again what I consider the basis of the formal educational process, the curriculum—that pattern of educational experience which brings together the expertise, ideologies, wishes, and confusions of educators as they try to meet the ambitions or ennui, the genius or academic weaknesses, the expectations and misconceptions of students. This is the realm in which the educator holds primary responsibility to himself and essential accountability to students. This is where the contract referred to by Dr. Powers is made. A curriculum is the ultimate statement education can offer. It is significant that we hear more today of programs than program budgeting.

This press toward a reconsideration of the essentials now focuses on the issues surrounding education and jobs. Education at all levels has been building a complex mythology around this relationship. Most recently it has emerged in that marvelous phrase "career education." Could any words sound more appealing to the ear of every parent, employer, student, administrator, and teacher? The myth runs like this: "Making a career decision is good. It is a primary goal of schooling. Such decisions should be made as early as possible. The career decision is an expression of personality and character. It gives social legitimacy and recognition. Educational institutions know about the range of career choices and know the components of each career. They can and will teach you about them or guide you toward them. If you make the decision well, you will move from school into the labor force quickly and easily."

In this oversimplified charge, the missing factor that makes the statement a cruel hoax is the fact that the availability of jobs and the composition of the employment market depend on the economy—not on education and certainly not on individual decisions. In the process of education, the availability of jobs is an independent variable. Today the composition of this available job mix changes more rapidly than ever before and is subject to acts of public policy. When the educational process is conceived of as career education, it addresses only the marginal aspects of the job issue. It deals with the top stratum of a very large pool of youthful unemployed people, a pool which has been growing steadily since the mid '50s in spite of years of affluence and prosperity. Jobs for the young and entry-level jobs in all sectors of the labor force have evaporated in the economic chill. Toward what educational essentials, then, are we being driven? I believe it is toward a recognition that the educational experience of pre-school, K to 12, college, and beyond has an integrity of its own. It is different from work—not unrelated, but different in a number of respects. The point of focus is the person, not manpower; individuals and the classifications are used only as a convenience. The educational contract, Dr. Powers notes, is voluntary, not required. It is open-ended, offering many promises and almost no guarantees. A content of the educational process is composed of things we know and things we don't know. One gives authority, but the other brings excitement. One builds stability, the other flirts with change. From these dualisms, one essential question arises, a birthright question for educators: How can the schools, particularly at the levels beyond tenth grade, strike a balance between educational integrity and career education?

This analysis of recent developments makes it clear that the curriculum is the focal point of most educational issues today. If there is an educational contract, then the curriculum is the statement provided by the party of the first part. In designing curricula, educators must be certain they would distinguish between what is known and what is not known; what can be done and what cannot be done. It is here that one difference with Dr. Powers' interpretation of generalizable education becomes clear. He proposes that we can move from the essentials of the work situation to the essentials of the educational experience. I maintain that the two are separate and that the educational experience has an integrity that must be developed by the curricular design.

I use the word "design" deliberately, for it embodies the notion of a total effect stronger than one might achieve simply by casting the pieces together randomly. The idea of design appears in two quite different frameworks. Engineering design emphasizes fitting together carefully constructed pieces, each with known characteristics. The artistic view of design begins with a total concept and achieves the effect not only by what is included but also by what is left out. The design of a curriculum can be approached by either route. Dr. Powers seems to be suggesting that we follow the first while my admonition is that we not neglect the second.

The Technical Side of Curriculum Design

Teaching what you know to a group of students is always challenging and intriguing, especially today when we have at our disposal a variety of instructional modes and a rich technology. In the setting of occupational education, the challenge has special significance because more and more young people will enter the labor force through an occupational route rather than through direct academic preparation. This was, of course, the normal channel for many decades. A review of the experiences of leaders in the generation just now retiring from active life will show that many of them spent a period of years following a basic education engaged in intermediate and often unrelated occupations. Lyndon Johnson, William O. Douglas, Hubert Humphrey, and Richard Nixon taught school or tended stores before moving on to law school.

We can expect increasingly that occupational education will be the medium of entry into a variety of advanced professional and business careers. The food industry, for example, can be generalized to the larger question of curriculum design. To begin with, technology is here to stay. Our society in its present form and in terms of its promise for human betterment depends heavily on it. The original meaning of the word "technology" emphasized the process of converting the knowledge and wisdom of science into practical application. That notion still lies at the heart of occupational education. The current problems attributed to technology arise because we approach the point where the various strengths of technological development interfere. One answer lies with an education that includes a sense of those limits in the process of learning. In the same way, the dehumanizing effects of technology can be dealt with by the refinement of what has been called "soft" technology to accommodate larger elements of personal consideration.

The kind of field experience embodied in the seminar-practicum described by Professor Powers illustrates the essential exchange process Max Weber saw as essential to the university. He conceived the basic disciplines as a core in constant contact with professional schools and practitioners. Problems that appeared at the practitioner level would be fed back to the core and the knowledge generated at the core would be quickly transmitted to the practitioners. This two-way exchange is vital, especially for education. One way to achieve it is to move students through a series of experiences that bring more elements of practice into play. Dr. Powers has provided several excellent illustrations. I would add a system that links the changing nature of the educational relationship to a particular kind of experience: as he moves from theory toward practice, a student first encounters *models* in which many of the variables are carefully controlled. A second instructional step, "guided design," is suggested by Professor Wales of West Virginia University. Here problems for study are carefully separated into graded parts. At each level, students confront an essential question and are encouraged to develop solutions by working in groups and individually. Once they explore the question, they are brought back to the central or "correct" position and then moved to a second level where the process is repeated. "Guided design," unlike models, introduces exploratory thinking as a practical, problem-solving tactic.

A third step in the movement toward practice is the use of case studies, which have the virtue of presenting simultaneously the kinds of variables a student may encounter on the job. Case studies pose no time constraints; students may linger over one or another aspect of the problem without risk. (In simulation and gaming, time becomes crucial; but even though the parameters are controlled, they can be moved to one extreme or another without threatening student participants.) On-site observation is the next step. Low risk participation, usually in marginal employment, follows. And finally, students participate in quasi-professional roles. Two educational questions need to be asked in connection with this sequence: (1) What is the best time to introduce each form of experience? and (2) What price does it exact from the other aspects of education? In his studies of the quality of life, Steven Withey has pointed out that the usual effects of a good college education, like higher voter participation, more community interest, and a wider range of personal activities, tend to diminish among those who are graduated from programs with a heavy occupational emphasis.

It is clear that some of the field experiences overleap the preliminary steps and move directly into low-risk job participation. Experience with students in a very good cooperative education program makes me appreciate the strengths and shortcomings. First of all, cooperative education works best when the state of technology and theory there is higher than it could be on campus. This is the case, for example, with computers and in engineering. It is true to a lesser extent in the business field and even less in economics and political science. Another consequence of the cooperative plan is that the curriculum must be rigidly structured to control administrative and instructional costs. And there is little flexibility in student scheduling. Cost of record keeping and liaison costs between the industry and the students are (if they are done right) substantial. Ignorance of this fact has undermined some otherwise promising programs. In summary, including field experiences in a curriculum design requires a careful assessment of the educational consequences and an understanding of both the costs and benefits to the student.

Keeping Tracks Open

One of the missions of American education has been to offer choices to students even as they move upward in the educational structure. Geographic, social, occupational, and intellectual mobility has been an implicit, if not explicit, goal of educational design. This commitment must be considered when one encounters the kinds of facts reported by Professor Powers. If there is to be an 80 percent growth in unskilled categories and a 90 percent growth in managerial categories, which direction does education take? Let us also assume that (as I expect) the entry into the field lies through the unskilled jobs into management. Should education provide people with entry-level training, understanding that those screened for managerial promotions will be retrained? Or should education keep a managerial perspective and accept the consequences of personal frustration among those who "don't make it." Is it sound to suggest that the amount of specialization should increase as people move higher on the educational ladder, as is the case in Europe?

There is an interesting dilemma here, and it is reflected in both Professor Powers' "generalizable education" and in my own distinction between the technical and critical components of education. In fact, the dilemma is often encountered but seldom acknowledged by schools that provide upper-level admission to students trained at the community colleges. Graduates with associate degrees in business have already had the basic accounting, basic marketing, and basic management courses that most four-year institutions offer. If a student has such technical training first, what should the upper division teach? Should it offer more specialized introductions to the technology of the field or should it attempt to move into a broader basis for practice in the occupation or profession? It seems apparent to me that curriculum design for preparation in the occupational fields must emphasize training at the entry level first, then gradually move toward a more generalized perspective on the profession and possible avenues of growth. If we accept that intermittent education—dropping out then dropping back in—is the wave of the future, then this approach seems to have validity. The move toward more generalized education at the advanced level seems to be implicit, too, in Dr. Powers' suggestion of base modules and flex modules. The food service industry, in one respect, offers an excellent illustration of another phenomenon that supports the notion of generalization at the higher levels. In gerontological programs and also in a number of other social service programs the catered meal becomes the social medium for communicating information, for diagnosing pathological conditions, and for organizing other activities. By designing curricula that move toward openness through more generalized study, we could open new pathways to these mixed careers.

In summary, the challenge facing us on the technical side of curriculum design is to respect the strengths of technology while acknowledging its shortcomings, build field experiences that do not compromise essential educational purposes, and maintain the openness expected of education. The curriculum designer must consider both the training needs of the occupational worlds and the educational needs of the students.

The Critical-Analytical Aspects of Curriculum Design

My thesis is that as schooling advances the emphasis should shift toward more generalized approaches. Technical material can be supplemented with other kinds of learning known to have long-range benefits.

First, introduction to uncertainty and engagement with the unknowns in the field become increasingly important. Higher education is not simply a matter of increased specialization or even of more elaborate problem solving. The advanced student should be able to handle the ambiguous, paradoxical, and speculative elements of the field; to acknowledge the problems; and to inquire into ways of dealing with them.

Second, we must pay attention to the existential qualities of the educational experience. Toward the end of his comprehensive study of inequality and the measured evidence related to it, Jencks observes that the qualities of the learning experiences that are immediately sensed—the feelings, the interpersonal reactions, the sense of self—may be much more important than we have been willing to concede. Advanced students should be encouraged to analyze the nature of their personal encounters with knowledge on several levels and thereby build their capacity to perceive the full dimensions of human experience, whether it occurs in the classroom or on the business site.

Third, some areas of knowledge (like languages) that have proved their validity over the span of human history become momentarily unpopular. It is the task of curriculum designers to maintain this rootstock. To sustain these areas they know to be sound, the designers must find ways of presenting the material in more significant forms. The tyranny of academic disciplines over student choice has its worst effect in creating a narrow vocationalism. Curricular designs that bring studies together around a central organizing principle have begun to appear—on a large scale at the John Jay College of Justice; on a smaller scale with programs like the study of North American French Culture at the College of Notre Dame in Manchester, New Hampshire. For those already well prepared in the technical side of their occupational fields, it should be possible to offer constellations of study that have a meaning of their own and draw, for coherence, upon literature, the social sciences, and professional fields.

Fourth, perhaps the greatest weakness on the non-technical side of education lies with the failure to name what we in education know to be happening. For example, large numbers of students enter pre-professional programs at the undergraduate level even though only a small percentage will actually reach professional school. The popular antidote for this situation is to introduce programs with occupational labels. In my view, there is a much better solution; but it presumes a sophisticated educational analysis of the undergraduate college experience that is not easily achieved. The curriculum would first be analyzed to identify all the understanding and skill competencies associated with the academic disciplines. (For example, history students would have to be adept at reading and writing, capable of making detailed analyses of documents, and able to fit immediate events into the perspective of the past. Psychology would require different competencies.) Students would construct a study program composed of competencies that reflect both abilities and interests. The program would include not only campus work but also outside experiences to enhance the competencies. Yet there would be no effort to link these studies with any occupational or professional area. It would, in fact, be carefully avoided so that the student could concentrate on his own development. By the time of graduation, instead of being narrowly prepared for a particular occupation, the student would possess a set of known competencies applicable to several different occupational groups. This design is not simply another version of "competency based learning" even though I am forced to use the term. The competencies I refer to are already present within the framework of the respective disciplines. What the curriculum design does is first to label them and second to realign them into significant constellations.

What emerges from both Dr. Powers' discussion and from this excursion into some of its implications is that those engaged in education from the tenth grade onward have a great deal of hard analysis ahead. The task is put into sharp focus by the words of C. Arnold Anderson: "The accelerating pace of technical change sharpens the tensions between what we must know and our anxieties over the kind of people we should become."

VI
Occupational Education, Higher Education, and a Changing Society

The Social Priority
of Adult Education

EDWARD V. ELLIS and MARLOWE FROKE

A quiet revolution in education began in the 1970s, and its basic tenet is the need for education throughout life. No person, this tenet holds, ever really completes his formal education. It must continue if he is to function productively in a complex society. The prodigious increase in knowledge, the interdependence of nations, and the impact of changing technology on all institutions require adult education.

Yet the concept of adult education is not really new. It has been accepted as an informal process since the birth of the nation. Social priorities and public policy, however, have always left responsibility for adult education with the individual himself. We have simply assumed that the opportunity for formal education would motivate a person to continue his learning by whatever means were available— whether they be public libraries, community cultural activities, or the use of his own money to pay for college.

The acceptance of this assumption has been almost universal, as witness the structures of almost all educational institutions and organizations: adult education is a concern of the libraries, museums, labor unions, businesses and industries, professional organizations, churches and synagogues, voluntary social clubs and associations, book publishers, and public and commercial broadcasters. It is a rare service or social club that does not have its "committee for education."

Chris DeYoung and Richard Wynn wrote that "adult education in this country has been characterized by a spontaneity, informality, and diversity of sponsorship that have made it adaptable to a vast spectrum of needs. However, this circumstance has resulted in a patchwork pattern that lacks central purpose and overall planning. Carried on by a motley miscellany of public agencies, . . . adult education has developed haphazardly along the route of its sponsors' self-interests."[1]

Whether it was self-interest or an intuition about satisfying a need not yet addressed in public policy is debatable. But operating within the framework of existing social priorities, organized education never really broached the issue in a systematic way. The initiative came from outside the educational system.

The quiet revolution in education proceeded, then, through a slow public acceptance of the concept of adult education and a methodical attempt to integrate it into the educational institution. It is this slow acceptance and the establishment of a social priority for adult education that will inevitably encompass the idea of "educating for new and emerging careers." There have been previous flurries of interest in this kind of education within the private and public educational sectors. But this interest usually centered on the satisfaction of some immediate need and flourished only insofar as the evolution of the entire educational system permitted systematic adult education.

Like all revolutions, quiet or noisy, this one has its antecedents. The Cooperative Agricultural Extension Service of the nation's land-grant colleges and universities was one. Established in 1914 under the Smith-Lever Act, the Extension Services amounted to a reordering of social priorities. This new allocation of federal, state, and local funds reflected the need of an expanding nation to disseminate information and education specifically to stabilize the food supply. The program was immensely successful; linked to the research arm of the agricultural programs in the land-grant universities (the "agricultural experiment stations") the Cooperative Agricultural Extension Services received much of the credit when the United States became the first major country to accomplish reliable food production and reserves. From the point of view of organized education, the effort could be faulted only semantically. The word "extension" suggests that the educational effort was ancillary rather than central. The actual process of instruction, while effective, followed the familiar adult education pattern: it lacked an organized, ongoing curriculum.

The land-grant universities—and later other institutions—subsequently applied the term "extension" to academic programs in other disciplines, changing the qualifier from "cooperative" to "general." General Extension thus became an academic function in those areas not already covered by Cooperative Extension. But, again, the choice of term falsely suggested that the function and the mission were not really central to education; though a service to be performed, extension was not among the high priorities of the educational institution or the nation.

Some later terms moved the concept of adult education into a position of somewhat higher educational priority. One of these new terms was "continuing education." It suggested the anachronism of the graduation ceremony as the termination of education. But it failed to marshal a consensus on its point of departure (continuing after what?) and gradually became synonymous with adult education.

As a term, "continuing education" is not unlike the later term "lifelong learning." Both imply the entire process by which society provides organized instruction for its people. Both embrace organized pre-school, elementary, secondary, and post-secondary education. And both imply, though they may not include, an organized, institutionally based educational system for adults. Adult education has yet to become a social priority approaching that of the rest of the educational system. Systematic programs of adult learning responsive to all the diverse needs and articulated with the other segments of organized education are not yet implemented. Adult education, then, is still unfinished business in this nation's educational system.

This lack of social priority produces conditions that deny the logic of lifelong learning. Thus lifelong learning and continuing education take on a more narrow meaning. The effort to draw the public's attention to this dilemma sometimes leads educators to slogans; "lifelong learning" thus joins other terms in the educators' verbal arsenal; and the revolution remains quiet even though some educators are sufficiently presumptuous—or optimistic—to discuss the "learning society" even as evidence of the need for organized adult education accumulates.

Borrowing on the success of the Cooperative Agricultural Extension Services, the nation attached to almost every piece of social legislation of the 1960s a provision for education or "training." If President Johnson's Great Society programs reflected a nation's attempt to solve some of its problems, they also reflected the conviction that education was an answer to those problems. Hundreds of short-term educational programs for adults were financed through social legislation. Millions of dollars were committed to one level of education or another. In 1972, the National Advisory Council on Extension and Continuing Education identified 168 such programs with more than a billion dollars allocated for continuing education by institutions of higher learning alone. But almost all aspects of these programs were aimed at solving short-term problems; thus their status was tenuous and their lives were short. They belied the fact that major educational goals cannot be achieved in brief periods. Quality education—its nature and its processes—cannot be shaped arbitrarily, especially in situations where an institutional structure from which to build does not exist. Policy makers did not realize that to achieve the types of success enjoyed by the Cooperative Agricultural Extension Services, substantial public funds for long-term educational planning, development, and evaluation were necessary. If only (went one argument) the legislators had placed all of the money from the diverse continuing education programs into one pot rather than parcel it out through hundreds of governmental agencies intent on pursuing short-range goals, the adult education system could have been established.

But it did not happen. Although the Higher Education Act of 1965 included a token appropriation at the federal level for "community service" for the institutionalizing of adult education, it was too meager to permit anything but piecemeal programs. And when the description was changed in 1976 to "continuing education and community service," it represented only a verbal refinement, not a substantial response to the basic public policy issue.

Two imposing conditions have, however, recently contributed to an awareness of adult education. The first is changing demographics. The second, born of the consumer movement, is a belief among some professional and occupational associations that education can provide some assurance that the public receives the quality of products and services it expects.

Demographics first: the birth rate dropped sharply in the 1950s and '60s, and the waves of young high school graduates entering post-secondary institutions are now subsiding. Some of these institutions have even had to close. Others have had to identify new student clienteles, among them those adults who because of work or family responsibilities or other circumstances cannot pursue an education full time.

Like adult education itself, this clientele is not really new. It has been served in the past by extension and continuing education. What is new is an awareness of the part-time adult student among those educators who heretofore concentrated on the full-time youthful learners. There has been no official enumeration of these older part-time students; until 1973, the Census Bureau did not even include people over 35 in its educational counts. The estimate then was 787,000 people over 35 in collegiate institutions. But by October of 1975, the Bureau estimate had risen to 1,183,000. Clearly, the rate of increase of part-time enrollments now far exceeds that of the young full-time students.

As a matter of survival, some institutions have begun recruiting adult students into programs originally designed for the 18 to 22 group. In their haste, however, they tend to overlook the research in the field of adult learning, instead justifying their recruiting on the untested assumption that learning is enhanced if one mixes all learners together, regardless of age, background, and experience. One can achieve certain results from such a mix, but these results are not central to adult education. In an unpublished study produced in 1976 for the U.S. Office of Education, James R. Broschart summarized some of the research in the field of adult education:

> If the adult is not enrolled formally as a fulltime student in an educational institution, he typically has multiple pursuits involving work, family, community, and individual interests. Thus, the adult has economic, domestic, and citizenship requirements that claim his time and attention.
>
> These two aspects—time and attention—are crucial [especially] when we add to this characterization of an adult the dimension of being a learning individual. We thereby generate specific and significant new conditions for learning that differ from those we attribute to children and youth. These new conditions are not only a function of the availability of time and attention, but they are also a result of the self-view an adult holds.

Drawing on earlier writings by Edmund Brunner, Broschart identified four major characteristics of the adult learner: self-concept, life experiences, readiness to learn, and orientation to learning.

Some post-secondary institutions are now sufficiently aware of the educational issues to distinguish between part-time and full-time learners. A few assign responsibility for the part-time learners to the continuing education function as a way of building on prior research and experience. Others, however, integrate these learners into the regular curricula solely as a means of saving the institution itself.

The second condition is a rush toward a form of mandatory continuing education in the occupations and professions. Its historical base rests on long established state licensing and certification practices involving those professions, like medicine, teaching, and the law, that affect the public welfare. Licensing and certification have, of course, spilled over into other occupations as a means of protecting the public against commercial practices that—although neither illegal nor harmful—constitute some abstract threat to the public's well-being. By 1975, one or more of the states licensed or certified some 32 occupations, including funeral directors, pawnbrokers, barbers, and poultry technicians.

Professional school education has been the traditional prerequisite for a license or certificate. But consumer charges that certain products and services were either inadequate or unnecessarily reserved to the certified practitioners produced the recent move toward relicensure and recertification. Because knowledge and practice change, the people who practice certain occupations and professions (it is said) ought to be continually reexamined. It is interesting to note that this pressure comes neither from the states nor from the educational institutions. It often comes, in fact, from the occupations and professions themselves through their societies and associations. By 1975, for instance, medical associations in 14 states had established continuing education as a condition for continued membership. And the practice has spread to other associations and professions. It has also spread to institutional employers: the American Hospital Association is considering a plan that would require each health care corporation to be responsible for the continuing competence of its employees.

Even while many of the occupations and professions seek to provide their own continuing education, however, consumer groups challenge the integrity of the education provided under these circumstances. As Phillip E. Frandson of the University of California points out:

> Traditionally it has been the universities that have had major responsibility in this area [and] the universities must be the primary implementing agency. They are the greatest single source of new knowledge in the professions, and by virtue of this, also the greatest single knowledge resource, through the faculties of their professional schools.
>
> In addition, the universities [have] an all-essential ingredient not found in any single professional association, the multi-professional viewpoint regarding the great issues of the day. The practice of medicine, for example, which has long involved the life sciences and physical sciences, now spills over into engineering, the law, management, and even the arts.
>
> I do not deny that the movement within some professional associations to develop their own continuing education programs is a healthy thing. . . . But if such programs are presented to state legislatures as evidence that associations should be solely responsible for continuing education, the potential for conflict of interest sanctioned by law is all too clear.[2]

The fact is that the occupations and professions are attempting to preempt some of continuing education, so Frandson's advice that the universities be allowed to set standards, plan, develop, present, and evaluate all aspects of continuing education programs leading to relicensing in the professions is wise. But some comfort can be taken from the history of licensure, at least in the medical profession. Decades ago, the Flexner Commission Report led to a system of medical school accreditation in order to abolish the diploma mills. And a state regulated licensure to establish minimum standards for medical practice resulted. The separation of the educational function from the actual practice of the profession has, therefore, proven to be sound. A similar separation should apply to continuing education.

One response to the recertification and relicensure issue rests in the conceptualization of continuing education or lifelong learning. Continuing education, after all, moves from the pre-college years through life; professional and occupational education moves over a much more limited span, as our figure illustrates. The process does not have to be so rigorously linear: a person might skip conventional college work for training in occupational or professional programs. That same person, subsequently motivated by his training and experience, might then enroll in an associate degree or baccalaureate program. This pattern can also accommodate a number of career changes, responding to the need for recurring education as an individual's interests change.

Because the concept of organized adult education is new, there has been a lack of appreciation of what it can mean to the already overburdened undergraduate curricula in a university's professional colleges. Rather than removing the liberal arts from a curriculum to accommodate the demand among students for professional preparation, the colleges could choose to defer some professional training to a time when a person who is already employed could return for further organized instruction.

As a practical response to the need for adult education, however, this approach appears to be a long way off. Current economic conditions portend diminishing tax support for "complete education" and its fifth component, adult education. Although latent support can be inferred from the extensive participation in various forms of adult education (most of it informal), elected officials feel no compulsion as yet to pass enabling legislation. Continuing education plans have been presented to some state legislatures, notably in California and Texas. And some state commissions established by federal law to

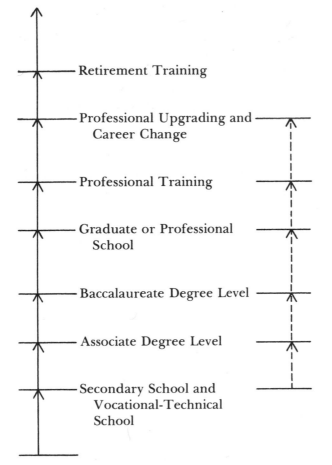

Retirement Training

Professional Upgrading and
Career Change

Professional Training

Graduate or Professional
School

Baccalaureate Degree Level

Associate Degree Level

Secondary School and
Vocational-Technical
School

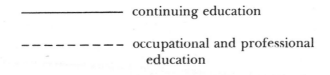

——————————— continuing education

– – – – – – – – occupational and professional
education

"coordinate" higher education have appointed continuing education committees or task forces. But these efforts have yet to produce tangible results.

Meanwhile, a few more phrases have been added to the lexicon of adult education. The "university without walls," for example, denotes a loose confederation of colleges and universities eager to accommodate adult students. It borrows its format from the British "open university," the distinction being that the British version is based on popular Labour Party policy. (Interestingly, the name "university without walls" implies that colleges and universities have built walls to exclude adults.)

A "University of Mid-America" has been created on paper to reflect emerging instructional technologies. But so far it is a university in name only. And some institutions have created "external degrees"—the choice of words again suggesting that adult education is outside the educational mainstream.

Only a few institutions have chosen to address some of the basic adult education issues.[3] But these few inevitably confront state legislatures not yet prepared to appropriate the funds necessary for faculties to plan, develop, and evaluate ongoing adult education curricula. So these questions remain: How long can society afford to wait before it extends to its adults the same social and economic support it grants its youth in this area? Should the financial base be the same as that provided for the rest of higher education—a portion borne by the state through public funds, the rest coming from participant payments? What financial aid should be provided for part-time students, who are often less able to pay than are full-time students? And how should adult education meet the problem of widely differing intellectual capabilities among adults learners?

That last question is particularly poignant. In 1971 in Pennsylvania alone, there were 3.5 million people of 16 years of age and older who had not completed and were not enrolled in high school. Moreover, of the 6.7 million adults in Pennsylvania over 25 years old, 50 percent had less than a high school education and 94 thousand had no schooling whatsoever. Though presumably a responsibility of the public school system, these illiterate and semiliterate citizens are, by public policy, effectively denied a chance for adult education. Yet the quiet revolution continues, its partisans insisting that the time for a public commitment to adult education has arrived. Educating some of these adults for new and emerging careers will certainly be inherent in the reordering of priorities that will attend the success of the revolution.

Notes

1. Chris DeYoung and Richard Wynn. *American Education,* 7th ed. New York: McGraw-Hill, 1972.
2. Phillip E. Frandson. "Continuing Education of the Professions: Issues, Ethics and Conflicts." *NUEA Spectator* 39, no. 21 (September 1975): 5–10.
3. John W. Oswald, President of The Pennsylvania State University, addressed these remarks to his Faculty Senate in 1972:

> There have emerged . . . in nearly all colleges and universities what now appears to be artificial and sometimes arbitrary rules and procedures separating students who are enrolled part-time from those enrolled for full-time study; students on campus from those off campus; students taught in the daytime from those taught in the evening; and students who learn independently from those who learn in classrooms. These rules tend to handicap students not only as they move from short-range to long-range educational goals, but also as they move to other colleges and universities throughout the state and nation.
>
> [We must] make available existing associate or baccalaureate degree programs to part-time students and, as time and resources permit, develop new ones. While this initial action would not assure the full establishment of extended degree opportunities, it would provide the enabling legislation under which the colleges could act responsibly.

Occupational Education, Higher Education, and a Changing Society

THOMAS F. POWERS

The liberal arts are thought to provide the least time-bound education of all because they address issues whose very timelessness prepares students for a changing world.

By contrast, many educators classify the recent surge in vocational
interest as a fad that will soon run its course. In a recent article, "The
New Vocationalism," James Hitchcock rehearses the trend toward
"relevance." In the late '60s, he asserts, the cult of relevance was
directed toward political awareness. But he suggests that the most
recent iteration of "relevance" is vocationalism.[1] The accompanying
table indicates, however, that an occupational interest among students
in higher education has developed right along with the growth in
higher education itself throughout the '60s and early '70s. The number of degrees awarded in the four occupationally related areas of
study shown in this table more than doubled in those 15 years. Thus
the growth in post-secondary occupational education that we are ex-
periencing represents a long trend, not just the current "in" thing.

Degrees Awarded in Selected Areas of Study

	1956–57	*1961–62*	*1966–67*	*1971–72*
Total bachelor's degrees awarded	311,298	420,485	562,369	594,110
Total by selected areas of study	152,171	178,540	226,272	356,732
Business and commerce	46,760	51,909	69,687	123,306
Education	77,722	97,507	120,879	192,368
Health professions	23,075	24,821	29,371	38,893
Home economics	4,614	4,303	6,335	12,165

Source: *Earned Degrees Conferred*, National Center for Educational Statistics.

Aside from the question of short- or long-run trends, many question the appropriateness of an increasing preoccupation with career preparation in higher education. Soon after I was graduated from college, an article appeared in *The New York Times Magazine* entitled "Education for All Is Education for None." It made enough of an impression that I remembered and recently unearthed it. It has a refreshing candor one rarely finds in the post-'60s egalitarian climate. The author begins,

> In schools, colleges, and universities today, the results of the huge increase in the student body suggests a rather painful thought: The principle of education for all, however fine in theory, in practice ultimately leads to education for none—if school standards are geared to an almost invisibly low average there is not much real education available for anyone, even for the gifted.
>
> The great problem has been and will be first the preservation of minority culture against the many pressures of mass civilization and, secondly, the extension of that minority culture to wider and wider areas. The rising flood of students is very much like the barbarian invasion of the early middle ages and then the process of education took a thousand years.[2]

In a society whose rhetoric has become a good deal more egalitarian, the problem is now viewed somewhat differently. In a recent article entitled "Higher Education or Higher Skilling," the author tells us that "more critically, colleges and universities have, for the most part, come to accept the role of training stations whose mission it is to turn out persons with marketable skills. *That* is the problem and the root of the crisis."[3] It is no longer fashionable to refer to the influx of students as barbarian waves—but we still deplore the fact that those students inevitably choose to study that which is of interest to them. The growth in our students' occupational interest *could* result in a narrow specialization in education, but that narrowness stems from inadequacies in the academic community rather than in the students. I will return to this point shortly.

Carl Kaysen has put the case for professional training in higher education with some eloquence. He points out that the

> elite culture of our society—one shared by leaders of most institutions of business, government and the professions—is the culture of rational problem-solving by the application of organized knowledge. . . . [T]he taste for knowledge and understanding for their own sakes is more likely to follow than to precede an appreciation of their instrumental power. The present sequence which puts liberal education before pro-

fessional training is more likely to be wrong than right. A real engagement with the intellectual effort that professional training demands is surer to stimulate the taste for learning in those in whom it has not developed than is a set of prescribed courses taken to meet the requirements for a degree. . . . What survives as a general education . . . in these circumstances is more likely to be of more permanent value.[4]

There has always been a tendency among some educators to equate civilization with the educational establishment and the highly educated. For them, education for all is indeed education for none. For them, the comfortable standards of an educational establishment serving an aristocratic society should be inviolate. Yet, in this Bicentennial year, let me note that, besides Washington, Adams, Jefferson, et al., the revolution had foot soldiers who believed in the prospect of their own liberty enough to fight for it. True, they seldom wrote about it. But from the first, our society drew its strength from the fullest participation of *all* its citizens. Now it is education's turn, particularly the turn of the two- and four-year colleges, to encourage this participation.

The "foot soldiers," the non-commissioned ranks of American society, are what Drucker calls knowledge workers.[5] And such other terms as "paraprofessional," "semi-professional," "foreman," or "unit manager" are also applied. Whatever the knowledge workers' title, our civilization is based on their individual productivity as it meshes with the various bodies of technical knowledge and social and real capital equipment in what Brzezinski calls our "technectronic society."[6]

Long ago John Dewey pointed out that the intellectual and social context in which occupational education presents itself had changed:

> The elements in industry due to mere custom and routine have become subordinate in most economic callings, to elements derived from scientific inquiry. The most important occupations of today represent and depend upon applied mathematics, physics, and chemistry. The area of the human world influenced by economic production and influencing consumption has been so indefinitely widened that geographical and political considerations of an almost infinitely wide scope enter in. It was natural for Plato to deprecate the learning of geometry and arithmetic for practical ends because, as a matter of fact, the practical uses to which they were put were few, lacking in content, and mostly mercenary in quality. But as their social uses have increased and enlarged, their liberalizing or "intellectual" value and their practical value approach the same limit.[7]

If Dewey's observation, made in 1916, had any merit in its day, clearly it ought to be generally accepted six decades later. We can assign the education of knowledge workers to some vocational limbo or bemoan the death of our culture only at our own peril. As we shape the education and socialization of these "foot soldiers," we affect the shape of our civilization in more fundamental ways than did the training and education schemes of earlier, aristocratic societies.

Indeed, there is a substantial population which higher education should be serving but is not, to both education's and society's loss. After pointing out that almost all of our very brightest high school graduates went to college in 1960, Jencks and Riesman go on to remark that

> from the bottom half of the social ladder less than half the men and a third of the women in the second ability quintile went to college in 1960. While some of these students certainly had poor high school grades, and some would have needed intensive help or a radically new sort of college to get them on their feet academically, many would not. It is among these students that there is currently most room for missionary work, assuming anyone can be interested in such unglamorous potential converts. It is the high schools' inability or unwillingness to encourage these students to attend college that accounts for the increasing importance of class background in determining which high school seniors go to college.[8]

The explosion in education's role in our society since the turn of the century has sprung largely from legislation and social policy. We required eight and then twelve years of school. But the growth in post-secondary occupational curricula and enrollments is a *voluntary* not a mandatory phenomenon. Voluntary phenomena in the United States are really "market phenomena," and the growth in post-secondary occupational enrollment marks higher education's move into mass society—and the mass market. These terms may repel some but they convey my meaning.

Once in the "mass market," education need not follow the consumer; but it can no longer ignore him—any more than Detroit could forever require us all to buy big cars. Nor will the demand for occupational education in baccalaureate institutions destroy the liberal fabric of education—unless educators permit it to do so by their own inability to respond to a new direction.

In thinking about occupational curricula, one should ask *where* people spend their lives. A very large part, of course, they spend at work. The enormous significance of work in determining not only the view society holds of a worker but also the view the worker holds of himself has been well documented.[9] If work is a central experience in life, the imaginative teacher with a properly constructed curriculum has the opportunity to address issues that heretofore have been accepted as the exclusive preserve of the liberal arts. Studies that relate knowledge to the students' life and work are what I had in mind when I earlier spoke of generalizable education.

In a course on management, the notion of a democratic and participative management style offers real meaning to the student who plans to be a supervisor, foreman, or manager. Notions of due process, either in union-management relations or in worker-management relations generally, may have more *real* application where the citizen-worker affects society than in abstract considerations of constitutional law. The notion of fairness in dealing with others and the basic issues of equity raised by the consumers' rights movement need not be considered simply a passing trend. They offer an instructor the opportunity to dramatize the value structure developed by our society as it can be operationalized rather than in the abstract.

In short, education is no longer exclusively for the elite who shape our society at the macro level. It now prepares foremen who will boss our children—and, for that matter, medical technicians who process the stuff of life and death. They can be callous and indifferent or warm and humane, according to the way education prepares them for their work. In a very real sense, their work *is* our society.

As occupationally oriented programs become a fact of life in higher education, the model of generalizable education should be used. But some frightening tales suggest that in some institutions this desirable goal gets abandoned in the swing from liberal arts to job preparation in its narrowest sense. The occupational goals of occupational programs in post-secondary and higher education are not served by narrow skill training. As Drucker points out, knowledge has become the key to productivity in our society. The systematic and purposeful acquisition of information and its systematic application are, he says, emerging as the new foundation for work, productivity, and effort throughout the world. In occupationally oriented post-secondary programs, the narrow, skill-based classes are out of place because of the rapid change in society and work alluded to earlier. Earl J. McGrath put the matter very well in a recent article in *Change:*

If the integrity and standards of a proper liberal arts college are to be preserved, career preparation must be of a character and level appropriate to an institution of higher education. Learning exercises consisting of repetitive how-to-do-it techniques and memorized facts hardly meet this standard. Instruction ought to be so grounded in theory as to achieve two indispensable goals of higher learning: first, it ought to provide sufficient general knowledge even in a technical field to enable the student to apply what he or she learns to the wide variety of circumstances in which it will later be needed; second, it ought to prepare students to extend their competence as new knowledge and skills emerge, and inculcate the habit of doing so.[10]

The Importance of Faculty

Throughout this discussion, I have stressed the importance of incorporating generalizable education into occupational curricula. A recent article, by James Hitchcock, however, sounded this important warning:

Advocates of the new vocationalism are no doubt sincere in asserting that it is not their intention that career programs be narrow and philistine, but that they aim for students, through practical disciplinary training, to learn useful skills and also to acquire the perspective and motivation to use them for the common good. But the long-term prospects are doubtful. Many professional persons are indifferent to larger social questions, not through moral failure or lack of intelligence, but because the time required to learn and maintain their professional abilities prevents them from acquiring a sophisticated awareness of larger issues.[11]

The danger the author notes is equally applicable to professional and paraprofessional educators.

The first qualification of any occupational instructor is a knowledge of the field—and appropriately so. This usually implies both theoretical knowledge and practical working experience. If we are to achieve generalizable learning in the occupational curricula, however, instructors' equipment must include the very general education we want them to incorporate in their curricula.

Too often in my own field of education I find instructors too preoccupied with the phenomena of our industry and simply not self-conscious about the fact that they are now working in the field of education. And I find, as well, a reluctance to evaluate the social significance of their work. As Dean Mattfeld of Brown University said recently, "Whether the education [students] are actually offered through formal instruction can be said to be 'liberal' will depend, in large part, on *how* they are taught those subjects they might choose to study."[12]

Jerome M. Ziegler, in a recent article, emphasized the importance of teacher training for higher education and advocated the establishment of centers or institutes for teacher training for higher education.[13] I would stress the need to insure that teacher training does not focus solely on narrow technical competence. The aim of such training should be to develop a teacher able to think of his field as problem-solving, rather than as a set of solutions, and able to understand the culture in which his students will mature.

If the best way for occupational education programs to deal with a changing world is to provide students with problem-solving tools rather than solutions, then we will need teachers who can view their subjects as dynamic processes rather than as static bodies of knowledge to be memorized and venerated. The key to education, then, is not just curriculum design that accommodates the future, nor simply the development of delivery systems that bring a current world into the classroom, nor even the effort to build general education experiences into occupational courses. These are all important, essential steps. But the key is to develop teachers capable of undertaking these assignments.

Notes

1. James Hitchcock. "The New Vocationalism." *Change,* April 1973, pp. 46–50.
2. Douglas Bush. "Education for All Is Education for None." *The New York Times Magazine,* 9 January, 1955, p. 13.
3. Steven Muller. "Higher Education or Higher Skilling." *Daedalus* 1 (Fall 1974): 148–58.
4. Carl Kaysen. "What Should Undergraduate Education Do?" *Daedalus* 1 (Fall 1974): 184.
5. Peter Drucker. *The Age of Discontinuity.* New York: Harper and Row, 1968, pp. 263–383.
6. Zbigniew Brzezinski. *Between Two Ages.* New York: Viking, 1970, pp. 9–23.
7. John Dewey. *Democracy and Education.* New York: Free Press, 1966.
8. Christopher Jencks and David Riesman. *The Academic Revolution.* New York: Doubleday, 1968, p. 143.
9. Anon. *Work in America.* Cambridge: MIT Press, n.d.

10. Earl J. McGrath. "The Time Bomb of Technocratic Education." *Change,* September 1974, pp. 24–29.
11. Hitchcock, "New Vocationalism," p. 50.
12. Jacquelyn Anderson Mattfeld. "Liberal Education in Contemporary American Society." *Daedalus* 1 (Fall 1974): p. 282.
13. Jerome M. Ziegler. "Some Questions Before Us: Notes Toward the Future of Higher Education." *Daedalus* 2 (Winter 1975): 210–21.

Contributors

Edward V. Ellis is associate dean for continuing education, College of Human Development, The Pennsylvania State University. He served as chairman of Penn State's Commission on External Degree Programs and helped to write its final report.

Marlowe Froke is director of media and of the learning resources center, Division of Continuing Education, The Pennsylvania State University. He served as secretary of Penn State's Commission on External Degree Programs and helped to write its final report.

Paul C. Gilmore is assistant to the vice president and chief scientist for the International Business Machines Corporation. He serves concurrently as an adjunct professor at Columbia University.

Nathan Glazer is professor of education and social structure at Harvard University and is co-editor of *The Public Interest*. He is the author of a number of books, the most recent of which is *Affirmative Discrimination*.

Thomas F. Green is professor of the philosophy of education and director of the Educational Policy Research Center at Syracuse University and president of the Philosophy of Education Society. He is the author of numerous articles on educational theory and policy and of the book *Work, Leisure and the American Schools*.

Edwin L. Herr is professor and head of counselor education at The Pennsylvania State University, president of the Association for Counselor Education and Supervision, and a member of the Board of the American Personnel and Guidance Association. He has written extensively in the field of counselor and vocational education.

Sheila M. Huff is a fellow at the Educational Policy Research Center, Syracuse Research Corporation, a group that engages in federal-level policy analysis. Currently a case study team leader in the NIE-sponsored evaluation of Title I, ESEA Administrative Practices, she has been Acting Director of the Task Force on Competency-based Education, sponsored by the Fund for the Improvement of Post-secondary Education.

Gary P. Johnson is associate professor of the economics of education, the Division of Education Policy Studies, The Pennsylvania State University. His research interests and publications have focused predominantly on the financing of post-secondary education.

Henry C. Johnson, Jr., is associate professor of the history of education, the Division of Education Policy Studies, The Pennsylvania State University. He is the author of a number of studies in educational history and theory.

Morgan V. Lewis is a senior research associate, Institute on Human Resources, The Pennsylvania State University. Several of his studies have been published by the Institute, including *The Role of the Secondary School in the Preparation of Youth for Employment: The Potential of Vocational Education* and *The High School Diploma: Credential for Employment?*

Al Lorente is an international representative, Skilled Trade Department, United Auto Workers, and vice president of the Michigan Career Education Advisory Committee.

Peter B. Meyer is associate professor of economic planning in the College of Human Development, The Pennsylvania State University. He is the author of numerous articles in the field of social accounting and cost and benefit analysis, to which he brings a socialist perspective. He recently published the book *Drug Experiments on Prisoners: Ethical, Economic, or Exploitative?*

Thomas F. Powers is professor of organizational behavior and professor in charge of the Food Service and Housing Administration Program in The Pennsylvania State University's College of Human Development. He has written extensively on the subject of paraprofessional education and recently completed a three-volume study on the future of the food service industry for the Research Coordinating Unit of the Pennsylvania Department of Education.

John R. Swinton is a research assistant in the Food Service and Housing Administration Program, College of Human Development, The Pennsylvania State University. His writing appears frequently in *The New York Times,* and he is associate editor of *Blindness Research: The Expanding Frontiers* published by The Pennsylvania State University Press.

Lester C. Thurow is professor of economics and management at the Sloan School of Management, Massachusetts Institute of Technology. He is the author of *Poverty and Discrimination* and *The American Distribution of Income.*

Kenneth S. Tollett is the director of the Institute for the Study of Educational Policy, Howard University. He is a lawyer and has served as dean of the Texas Southern University School of Law. He has been a visiting fellow at the Center for the Study of Democratic Institutions and is a member of the Carnegie Commission on the Future of Higher Education.

William E. Toombs is assistant director of the Center for the Study of Higher Education and associate professor of higher education at The Pennsylvania State University. He recently contributed a chapter, "New Colleges for New Occupations," to *Land Grant Universities and Their Continuing Challenge,* edited by G. Lester Anderson.

Arthur G. Wirth is professor of the history of education, Graduate Institute of Education, Washington University. He has written widely on the progressive movement in education and is author of the book *Education in the Technological Society: The Vocational-Liberal Studies Controversy in the Early Twentieth Century.*

Helen D. Wise is a social studies teacher at the Westerly Parkway Junior High School, State College, Pennsylvania. She is also a trustee of The Pennsylvania State University and a past president of the National Education Association. In 1976 she was elected to the House of Representatives of the Pennsylvania General Assembly.

Index